EATING LAS VEGAS

EATING LAS VEGAS

THE 52 ESSENTIAL RESTAURANTS

John Curtas

HUNTINGTON PRESS
LAS VEGAS, NEVADA

EATING LAS VEGAS

The 52 Essential Restaurants

Published by
Huntington Press
3665 Procyon Street
Las Vegas, NV 89103
Phone (702) 252-0655
e-mail: books@huntingtonpress.com

ISBN: 978-1-944877-11-8
$14.95US

Production & Design: Laurie Cabot
Cover Photo: Wing Lei at Wynn Las Vegas ©Barbara Kraft
Special acknowledgment to Tazeen Shazreh Ahmed who served as the official photographer for this edition.

Inside Photos: Spoon ©Torsten Schon, Dreamstime.com; La Cave Wine & Food Hideaway: vi; MGM Resorts International: x, 30, 74, 76, 78, 84, 88, 90, 96, 104, 106, 114, 161, 168, 179, 240; Cosmopolitan of Las Vegas: 8, 36, 58, 64, 70, 132, 156, 166, 173, 185, 219; Tazeen Ahmed: 22, 134, 140, 143, 149, 150, 152, 153, 165, 171, 175, 177, 180, 182, 188, 190, 192, 199, 202, 205, 213; Venetian/Palazzo: 24, 34, 40, 217; Wynn Las Vegas/Robert Miller: 26; Andrés Bistro & Bar: 28; SLS Las Vegas: 32, 159; Botecto/Alessandra & Marcus Fortunato: 38; MGM Resorts International/Douglas Friedman: 42; Vox Solid Communications: 44, 66, 178; Peter Harasty: 46; Chica Las Vegas: 52; Chada Vegas: 52, 222; Jeff Green: 54; District One: 56, 151; EATT Gourmet Bistro/Nicolas Kalpokdjian: 60, 164, 220; Elia Authentic Greek Taverna: 62; Hiroyoshi Japanese Cuisine: 68; Japanerio: 72; Kabuto: 80; Khoury's: 82; Wynn Las Vegas/Barbara Kraft: 86, 124, 169; Bill Hughes: 92, 140; Marche Bacchus: 94; Venetian/Palazzo/Jerry Bacon: 98; Caesars Entertainment: 100, 160, 162, 164, 210; Amanda B. Lee: 102; John Curtas: 108, 139, 141, 146; Caesars Entertainment/Scott Roeben: 110; Jenny Quinn: 116; Trattoria Nakamura-Ya: 118; Mandarin Oriental/Bread & Butter Public Relations: 120, 130; Urban Turban/Bhushan Arolkar: 122; Greg Thilmont: 126; Yuzu Kaiseki/Mayumi Azeuchi: 128; Chubby Cattle/NXT-Factor: 136; Boyd Gaming/Ping Pang Pong: 142, 212; Mon Restaurant Group: 144, 145, 193; Jasper Ibe: 147; Mother's Korean Grill: 148; Crown Bakery: 154; Island Malaysian Cuisine: 154; Snowflake Shavery: 155; One 7 Communications: 158; Ellis Island: 161; Delices Gourmands French Bakery: 163; Burger Bar Las Vegas: 170; Fat Choy: 172, 196; White Castle: 174; Caesars Entertainment/Anthony Mair: 176; Amoré Taste of Chicago: 181; Pizza Rock Las Vegas: 183; Border Grill/Matt Armendariz: 184; Frijoles & Frescas Grilled Tacos: 186; Lindo Michoacan: 187; Tacos Mexico: 189; Sojo Japanese Restaurant: 191; Bill Milne: 194; John Mull's Meat & Road Kill Grill: 197; Lola's-A Louisiana Kitchen: 198; Roma Deli & Restaurant: 200; Sin City Smokers: 201; Bootlegger: 203; Golden Steer Steakhouse: 203; Peppermill Restaurant and Fireside Lounge: 206; Pioneer Saloon: 207; Capriotti's Sandwich Shop: 208; Krung Siam Thai: 211; Giordano's: 215; Andiamo Steakhouse: 216; MGM Resorts International/Gavin Rosedale: 218; Violette's Vegan & Kira Caraway: 221; Lotus of Siam: 226; Sparrow + Wolf/Sabin Orr: 232; Bryan Adams: 241

Dedication

For my sons Anthony and Alex—the fruit of my loins and the apples of my eye and the best damn dining companions any father ever had.

CRAB WRAPS AT LA CAVE

Contents

Section I–The 52 Essential

Section II–Additional Recommendations

Section III–Index and Maps

ZUPPADI PESCE AT CARBONE

Introduction

> "In the lexicon of lip-smacking, an 'epicure' is fastidious in his choice and enjoyment of food, just a soupçon more expert than a 'gastronome'; a 'gourmet' is a connoisseur of the exotic, taste buds attuned to the calibrations of deliciousness, who savors the masterly techniques of great chefs; a 'gourmand' is a hearty bon vivant who enjoys food without truffles and flourishes; a 'glutton' overindulges greedily, the word rooted in the Latin for 'one who devours.'
>
> "After eating, an epicure gives a thin smile of satisfaction; a gastronome, burping into his napkin, praises the food in a magazine; a gourmet, repressing his burp, criticizes the food in the same magazine; a gourmand belches happily and tells everybody where he ate."
>
> —William Safire

There comes a time when all you want is the best. It arrives after years of leg (and stomach) work, having slogged many meals over many *many* miles.

In the beginning, you're an omnivore—a gourmand, if you will—eating everything in sight, building up a culinary catalogue in your head (and palate) of every taste, every flavor, every texture you encounter with every bite. At first, you don't even know you're doing it; you just want to devour everything and learn as much about it as you can. But after you've eaten everything from fish tacos in Cancun to bouillabaisse in Marseille, the quest for quintessence is all you seek, be it in a burrito, a burger, or a Béchamel.

Becoming an epicure is no easy task. It takes years—decades, really—of eating, reading, cooking, traveling, and tasting. Anyone who thinks you can become a gourmet simply by eating in restaurants is a fool. You can no more learn about food by eating in a lot of restaurants than you can learn about music by attending a lot of concerts. Great restaurant meals are the payoff for all your hard work, and the older you get, the more you want to maximize your enjoyment of them.

When you're in your omnivorous stage, the world is your oyster. An obscure pho parlor is as fascinating as an out-of-the-way taco truck. But the moment you realize there's more time behind you than ahead, you're no longer interested in exploration, only in excellence.

This 6th edition of *Eating Las Vegas* is the result of my 27 years of searching for excellence in the Las Vegas food scene. It's the culmination of more meals than I can count (consider 10 restaurant meals a week times 50 weeks a year times 25 years and you'll get the idea), more calories than I need, and more tiramisu than any man should eat in a lifetime. But I've loved every minute of it. Even the bad meals have taught me something, and the ethereal life-changing epiphanies I've had in Las Vegas restaurants—Paul Bartolotta's roasted wild turbot, a 14-month-old "riserva" steak at Carnevino, green-sauce chicken at Chengdu Taste, every bite I've ever had at Restaurant Guy Savoy—I wouldn't trade for the world.

To be sure, much is lacking in our food scene—agriculture being first and foremost. Ours is a top-down industry, enabled solely by the marketing muscle of the casino industry. Make no mistake, there's nothing "organic" about our restaurants. If not for the revolution wrought 20-plus years ago by Wolfgang Puck, Steve Wynn, Sheldon Adelson, and others, Las Vegas would still be the home of cheap prime rib and mountains of (frozen) shrimp cocktails. This is one of the reasons we get routinely ignored by the James Beard Foundation, which reveres the suffering-for-their-art chefs and looks upon our eateries as bloated, overstuffed, food factories for the Branson, Missouri, crowd.

True enough, no chefs working on the Strip—be they at Guy Savoy or Bobby Flay's Burger Palace—are suffering for any art. At most, they're well-paid functionaries of the corporations that employ them. Indeed, very few are suffering for anything, except the constant pressure of trying to please their masters, avoiding sleep deprivation, and feeding the demands of 43 million hungry tourists a year.

But this book isn't interested in the mouths of those 43 million. It's

interested in *you*, reading these words. Because if you care enough to get this far in this introduction, you clearly have a certain dedication to eating well. And eating well, as in eating the best food in Las Vegas, is what this book is all about.

Yes, it's a guidebook, but of more limited scope than many. If you expect a comprehensive tour of Las Vegas restaurants, look elsewhere. If you want to know whether some obscure (usually terrible) Italian place in some third-rate hotel is worth your dining-out dollar, consult Yelp, Thrillist, TripAdvisor, or any number of websites devoted to crowd-sourced opinion.

This book is as far from crowd-sourced opinion as you can get. We've seen the crowd; we've listened to the crowd; we've even been (on occasion) friends with the crowd; and you, my friend, should know that the crowd is generally full of beans when it comes to judging the best of the best. The crowd hasn't eaten in a restaurant every year for a decade to see how it evolves; the crowd hasn't observed subtle changes from chef to chef; the crowd can't tell when that baguette is 30 minutes past its peak condition or that gelato has been kept at a few degrees south of perfect refrigeration. The public, God bless them, is concerned about bang for the buck. Yours truly, you need to know, doesn't give a fuck about bang for the buck.

No, all I care about is quality, quintessence, perfection—be it in a haunch of beef or a bunch of broccoli. Price isn't disregarded altogether, but comparing buffets isn't my interest or mission statement. (I leave that to the *Las Vegas Advisor* in the back of the book.) Telling you whether to drop a house payment at Joël Robuchon or a car payment at Bazaar Meat is what this tome is all about. If you're looking for the best Szechuan food in Chinatown, you've come to the right place. Best burgers in town? Step right in. If quintessential (expensive) Japanese floats your boat, we're here to help. On the other hand, if AYCE sushi is what you're after, you have our sympathies.

The great thing about the Las Vegas food scene is its variety. Only New York City has more great steakhouses and our top-shelf Italians exceed almost any city's other than the Big Apple. Washington, D.C., and Dallas have thriving food scenes, but try finding a fancy French restaurant there. Portland may have more gastropubs and greater Los Angeles can't be beat for Asian eateries, but if you're looking for across-the-board quality, Sin City caters to all types and caters to them well.

To recap, let's review the pros and cons of eating Las Vegas, to both inspire and warn you about what's really going on around here.

Pros

Fabulous French—As mentioned above, most American cities, outside of New York, are lucky to have one or two good French restaurants. We have 10.

Great steaks—Boffo beef abounds in our burg.

Incredible Italian—There are very good Italian restaurants in Vegas (Bratalian, Buddy V's, Rao's, Portofino) that didn't make the cut in this book.

Terrific Thai—Even our mediocre Thai restaurants, dozens of them, are pretty good. The top three in town—Chada Thai, Chada Street, Lotus of Siam— sport world-class wine programs on par with their incendiary cooking.

Amazing Chinatown—Cheap and tasty eats abound only a mile west of the Strip. Leave your timidity behind and you'll have a feast for four for the price of a couple of cocktails at the Wynn/Encore.

Everyone's turning Japanese—In the past decade, righteous ramen, pullulating udon, exciting Edomae sushi, and great gyoza have invaded Chinatown. Be advised: The best stuff is in the 'burbs. Big-box Japanese, such as Nobu, Hakkasan, and Morimoto, are soooo 2010. The only people eating in them these days are vinyl-siding salesmen from Kansas.

Broad and deep wine lists—But at a price. See below.

Something for everyone—There are more good eats at the Aria Hotel than there are in any mid-sized city in America. The food at Aria can satisfy everyone from Granny to the fussiest gastronome. And it's not the only hotel in Vegas that can make this claim.

Great service—Bad service on the Strip is almost non-existent.

Easy access—Make a reservation or just show up; someone will bust his or her ass to find you a seat.

No attitude—You won't find "mission statements" or "bad-boy-doing-it-his-way" chefs in Las Vegas.

Understandable food—See above.

Comfort—Strip restaurants never contracted the tiny-tables shitty-chairs virus that infects most hipster haunts in say, Seattle, D.C., or Brooklyn. The chairs are padded and the air conditioning always works.

Adult noise levels—A few joints around town are ear-splitting at

prime times, but for the most part, you can hear yourself think while you're eating. Even Batali has toned down his tunes.

Great cocktails—Ever since the cocktail revolution took hold about a decade ago, it's been hard to get a bad drink in a Vegas hotel. Or even off the Strip, for that matter.

Top-shelf ingredients—Our best restaurants get meat, fish, and veggies on par with anyone's. True, 99% of it flies or drives to get here, but Chicago chefs don't exactly have fish jumping out of the ocean and onto their stoves either. Those vaunted New York sushi bars charging an arm and a leg for their omakase are getting the same fish, from the same Tokyo purveyors, as Yui and Kabuto are. And the bounty of California is a lot closer to us than it is to Atlanta.

People-watching—If you don't love people-watching in Vegas, you're either vision-impaired or not paying attention.

Sweet release—The pastry talent in Vegas is legendary. I'll stack the desserts coming out of our finest restaurants up against any, anywhere, anytime.

Cons

No imagination—If you're looking for highly personalized chef-driven food, look elsewhere, or off the Strip. With a few notable exceptions (our fabulous frog ponds being first and foremost), Vegas restaurants are food factories pure and simple. More than one chef has had his ambitions and enthusiasm crushed under the weight of feeding 500 picky eaters a day.

Overpriced wine—Las Vegas wine lists are best approached with a soothsayer, accountant, mortgage banker, and defibrillator on hand. A jar of K-Y jelly helps too. You'll also pay extra for that reach-around.

Overpriced drinks—The Strip is home to the $15 cocktail … which is fast becoming the $20 cocktail.

Incredibly bad Italian—Las Vegas is home to more terrible Italian restaurants than any city in the country. Amerigo Vespucci must roll over in his grave every night thinking of the slop being served in the name of his homeland in the land that he named.

Corporate soul-crushing sameness—Every goddamn restaurant in every goddamn hotel serves a pizza, and a pasta, and a salmon, and a chicken, and a steak, and a (bad) Caesar salad. Throw in a couple of trendy items like sliders, kale, bone marrow, and pork belly and you have your instant, interchangeable, eating experience! Reading

Las Vegas menus is like living in an endless loop of a Guy Fieri fever dream.

Hoi polloi—Cargo shorts (men) and yoga pants (women) are everywhere. Usually on people with asses too big to be wearing them. Speaking of asses …

Asses with money—Las Vegas is not, I repeat, not a gambling town; it's a convention town. Asshole gamblers throw money around like it's confetti; asshole conventioneers are livin' large for 3.5 days on the corporate credit card. Gamblers know how to behave in public; Middle Manager Mike from Milwaukee acts like he's never seen cleavage or a cote de boeuf before. Which he probably hasn't.

Celebrity chefs—I'm of two minds about celebrity chefs. On the one hand, our amazing restaurant scene wouldn't exist without them. If not for the corporate-branding ambitions of Mario Batali, José Andrés, Wolfgang Puck, Michael Mina, et al., we'd still be living in prime rib purgatory. Twenty-five years ago, they saw gold in them thar hills and saved me from a life of "gourmet rooms," Continental cuisine, and coffee shops. On the other hand, many of them (not the four mentioned above) use Vegas like a late-night booty call for cash. Don't fool yourself: The only reason Giada, Morimoto, Gordon Ramsay, Bobby Flay, or Alain Ducasse show up twice a year is because they're contractually obligated to. The restaurants themselves are owned and run by the hotels.

Comps—Here's how comps work. You blow a lot of money gambling. The casino then gives you a voucher for something "free," usually a meal. You go to the restaurant to eat for "free." No money changes hands at the restaurant, but to ensure that you use up that comp as fast as possible, the restaurant (owned by or in cahoots with the hotel) charges insane markups. Everybody wins! Except those who pay with their own money and expect a fair exchange. I once saw a quartet of young Asian men stroll into a joint and sit down at a table with four bottles of Cristal champagne on each corner and a bowl of caviar the size of a basketball in the middle. They spent exactly ten minutes at the table, talked on their cell phones the whole time, and left without eating a thing. I paid $343 for my meal.

No one gives a shit about you; you're just a number—And when you leave, 10 more just like you are waiting for that seat. When you consider the numbers they do—a million a month in gross receipts is average—it's amazing how cordial Strip restaurants are. Most could act like carnival barkers when dealing with their ever-clamoring customers and still get away with it.

Food-and-beverage executives—There are exceptions (Bellagio,

Mandalay Bay, and SLS, to name a few), but the "company-man" mentality that runs the F&B programs at most hotels is always threatening to turn Vegas into an armada of predictable franchised grub. Which works fine if you're a glorified accountant. Which most of them are.

Size matters (as long as it's big)—Most Vegas restaurants are behemoths. A 175-seat joint is average; places like Carnevino and Bazaar Meat seat more than 300. Intimate they're not. If you want intimacy, go to Le Cirque ... or San Francisco.

Expense—Make no mistake: Vegas is the most expensive restaurant town in America. The mantra of the big hotels is "hit 'em hard, hit 'em fast, and wait for the next sucker to show up." The down-pricing and bargains instituted during the Great Recession are but a dim memory now. Sticker shock is everywhere; even the buffets will set you back a Benjamin (for two) these days. Big-city gourmands gasp when they see the cost of a prime steak or bottle of Cabernet out here. Personally, I go to other big cities (New York, L.A., Paris, Rome) when I want to dine well for less money. There's a lot of fantastic food in Las Vegas, but you'll pay through the nose for it.

The Way It Is

So, that's your yin-and-yang snapshot of all that's fascinating, good, bad, wonderful, and infuriating about my beat, the pavement I've pounded day and night for a quarter-century now. This book is my most personal one yet and the most unfettered when it comes to my opinions. Gone are the co-authors with whom I battled mightily over the inclusion or exclusion of restaurants from these pages. This is where I love to eat in Las Vegas and why. Nothing more, nothing less. It is all about the best and nothing else. If the best eating in Vegas is what you seek, you've come to the right place.

Price Designations

At the top of each review is one of four price designations: $25 or less, $25-$75, $75-$125, or $125 and up. They provide a general guide to what it will cost you to dine there, based on the per-person price of an appetizer, an entrée, a side or dessert, and one or two lower-priced cocktails.

CAVIAR, OYSTERS, AND MORE AT BLUE RIBBON

Evolution of a Restaurant Critic

Food writer John Mariani once categorized three kinds of restaurant critics: "The slobs, the snobs, and the oh-goodie-goodies."

The slobs are professional writers who either get thrown into, or decide to write about, food sometime in mid-career. Being writers by trade, their qualifications for the gig (when they start out) usually consist of being able to write a cogent paragraph and knowing what they like to eat. Any editor will tell you a real writer who wants to become a food critic is preferable to a passionate foodie who wants to (try to) become a writer. Getting real writers to write about restaurants is usually a lot easier than getting them into a collared shirt.

Mariani properly pegged me as an "oh-goodie-goodie" type of critic years ago. For the longest time, I ate everything in sight and was pleased as punch that Las Vegas was taking its place on the world's gastronomic stage. Somewhere over the past decade, I shed my omnivorous obsessions and replaced them with unabashed epicurean snobbery, and therein lies the tale.

John Anthony Curtas was practically raised in American restaurants. As a preteen in the 1960s, I circumnavigated the United States with my family, eating in the best restaurants from Miami to Seattle, New York to New Orleans. My parents were hardly "to the menu born," but both had a healthy appreciation for good food and wanted their children (two sisters, a brother, and I) to experience the best of eating out. Neither parent was a gourmet; we never had wine or liquor in our house and seafood was as foreign to our table as chopsticks. But Mom and Dad loved going out to a restaurant—dressing us all up and making a night of it. To them, dining out was about the experience of leaving the confines of home and seeking the thrill of being served good food in a fabulous place where they waited on you hand and foot. Wherever we traveled, they always sought out the best restaurant in town and the best table in the house, the better to experience the theater of great dining.

As a young adult, I started cooking more out of poverty than choice. My older sister gave me a subscription to *Bon Appetit* magazine in 1978 that I ate up, literally and figuratively. An early girlfriend and the second Mrs. John A. Curtas were both foodies before such a term existed and they indulged my then-passion for Chinese food. By 1980, I'd pretty much cooked my way through *The Chinese Menu Cookbook* (Joanne Hush and Peter Wong, Holt Rinehart Winston, 1976) and was seduced by the Szechuan craze that was all the rage then. (Yes, there was a Szechuan craze in those prehistoric times and I have the cookbooks to prove it.)

My ex-wife was even so kind as to compile a list of Chinese grocery stores for me when we first moved to Vegas in 1981, so I could continue working my way through the various regional cuisines. Until around 1990, if you'd asked me what my favorite food in the world was, I would've answered the strong, salty, sour, and hot foods of the Szechuan and Hunan provinces of China. (Then and now, the textural nuances of Cantonese cooking and the folderol of Mandarin banquets remain more of a curiosity than a keen pursuit.)

Wedged into all of this was a move back east in the mid-1980s, where I lived a mere 50 miles from midtown Manhattan. It was a seminal time for American food and I consumed the New York restaurant scene wholesale, as Danny Meyer, Drew Nieporent, Larry Forgione, et al. developed a food-centric, wine-friendly, customer-casual template that put Baby Boomers at ease with sophistication without pretense.

In 1990, after five years of eating in places like Odeon, the Coach House, Four Seasons, Peter Luger, and the Union Square Café (not to mention enjoying the best seafood in America every summer on Nantucket), I moved back to Las Vegas and surveyed the edible landscape. It was not a pretty sight. The best restaurants in town were two chain steakhouses: Ruth's Chris and Morton's. Every hotel had five eateries: coffee shop, buffet, steakhouse, Italian, and a (not very) "gourmet room" serving "continental cuisine" from some unnamed continent. All of them faced the keno pit, or so it seemed. Marcel Taylor, the Caesars Palace dealer who brought Ruth's Chris to town in 1989, told me that the philosophy of every hotel back then was to capture casino customers and never let them out the front door. As he put it, "We had every place to eat right there. What more could the tourists want?"

But want they did, and when Ruth's Chris realized its Las Vegas outpost was outselling all its other franchises, the word quickly spread to upscale chains and chefs everywhere that Vegas was the place to be. Late 1992 brought the opening of Wolfgang Puck's Spago; soon thereafter Mark Miller, Charlie Trotter, and Emeril Lagasse planted their flags in the MGM. Suddenly, we had a real restaurant scene.

The only thing lacking was a serious critic to write about it. It might be hard to believe 24 years later, but in 1994, the only person covering restaurants in Las Vegas was the mother-in-law of a certain newspaper owner. She belonged to the "My friend Mabel had the chicken soup and she thought it was a bit salty" school of food writing and was avidly followed every week by the few society matrons in town.

So I stepped into the breach. It took a year of hounding media outlets, but finally in October 1995, I got a shot at being the Nevada Public Radio food critic, a position I pretty much invented for myself and a gig that lasted until 2011. Did I know anything about radio? Absolutely not. But I knew a helluva lot about food, could put two sentences together, and looked great in a button-down shirt. As I like to say: In the land of the blind, the one-eyed man is king.

For five years, I was the only game in town when it came to critiquing serious restaurants in a serious way. It wasn't until 2001 that our main newspaper hired a full-time food writer and, in keeping with tradition, they made sure she was of the "My friend Edna had the steak and she thought it was a little chewy" school of food writing.

The '90s brought multiple trips to France and Italy and writing for all sorts of magazines and guidebooks. That was when I honed my palate and my writing. It took a decade-plus, but only after all those meals, reviews, and plane rides did I begin to appreciate my subject matter and my relationship to it.

Food is the most intimate relationship we will ever have and allowing strangers to cook it for us is an oddly perverse ritual that many struggle to understand. (It's the reason so many people have a chip on their shoulder when they eat out.) Giving over our bodies, our health, and our mouths to persons unknown and paying them for the privilege of feeding all three is surrendering an inordinate amount of power to a stranger. This curious dynamic continues to fascinate me as much as anything that I shove in my piehole.

As for the food, then and now the ingredient-driven Italians and technique-driven French have always intrigued my palate. French food—more than any other on Earth—is impelled by the extraction, concentration, and layering of flavors. Italian cuisine, in all of its regional glories, celebrates the simplicity of the raw material, while French cuisine tries to make it taste even more like itself. The yin and yang of these philosophies still hold me in their thrall and, of course, the French and Italians both make the best wine on the planet (sorry Spain and California).

Enter Japan. Japanese food is about the quest for perfection and in many ways, eating Japanese food in the U.S. and Japan has refined my tastes even further and eliminated my helter-skelter insatiability. No longer am I a galloping gourmand, happily ingesting everything in sight. Now in my sixties, I seek the unobtainable grail of the quintessential. Like a Japanese chef, I take interest in the details of the divine. A wasted meal, or even an ingredient, puts me in a bad mood. I've eaten so much of everything that I now simply want the best of anything, be it in a street taco, a glass of wine, or a piece of fish.

I'm no longer an "oh-goodie-goodie" and I'm certainly not a slob. It's said that to become a gourmet, like becoming a first-class horseman, you have to start young. I'm an epicure and I did start very young. But many more steps are ahead of me and it's this mountain that I continue to climb.

The Job of a Restaurant Critic

Eat. Write. Cook. Travel. Eat more. Study. Read everything possible about food and travel. Eat even more.

Most of all, restaurant critics think incessantly about food. Not just the food that their happens to be forking into their faces at any one moment, but about how everyone eats. And cooks. And feeds one another. More specifically, restaurant critics are charged with the responsibility of evaluating how businesses that sell food to satisfy some human urges—hunger primarily, but also the quest for quality, value, exotica, novelty, or distinction—are doing their job.

To be a good restaurant critic, you need to eat a lot, write a lot, read a lot, and travel a lot. If you lack the stamina for any one of these things, you should hang it up right now. It's like being a porn star: It sounds like great idea until you have to do it all the time, on schedule.

Restaurant critics (real ones, not casual food bloggers) are writers first and foremost. But their beat isn't sports or news or politics, it's rating and reviewing each and every morsel of a meal they ever put in their mouths, then putting those thoughts on paper or screen, usually weekly, facing deadlines.

Secondly, restaurant critics are consumer advocates. If your motivation for the job isn't to help the general public spend their dining dollars wisely, you should find another occupation. People who just like to eat out all the time and tell everyone what they think of their meals are known as blowhards ... or food bloggers. Food bloggers, as knowledgeable and passionate as some of them are, aren't restaurant critics.

Real restaurant critics get paid for what they do.

There are four types of professional critics: 1) full-time columnists who write for major metropolitan newspapers or national periodicals (these jobs are becoming increasingly rare, there are probably fewer than 100 people in America who make a living this way); 2) freelance journalists who subcontract to magazines, free newsweeklies, and daily newspapers, sometimes as a steady gig, sometimes intermittently; 3) online critics who work for large websites (like Grub Street, Eater National, and Huffington Post); or 4) established critics who maintain their own websites (some are monetized, some aren't). As for me, I fit into the second category for the first 15 years of my restaurant writing career and now ply my trade as a member of the fourth group, with occasional forays into numbers 2 and 3.

Restaurant critics don't make a lot of money. If you're lucky enough to land a job with a newspaper, you'll make about as much as a schoolteacher; if you freelance, you'll be lucky to top a barista at Starbucks. It's like being a poet: You do it for the love of your subject or you don't it at all. And like dedicated poets, you should always remember what Robert Graves said: "There's no money is poetry, but then there's no poetry in money either."

Food writers aren't restaurant critics. A food writer pens articles or books about food. A food writer might write an entire book about a specific food topic, such as *Salt* by Mark Kurlansky, or on diet and food politics, for example *The Ominvore's Dilemma* by Michael Pollan. For food fads, pick up any monthly food magazine like *Bon Appetit* or *Saveur*. Food writers also write about themselves (M.F.K. Fisher), or recipes (Julia Child), or travel (Anthony Bourdain, Joseph Wechsberg, etc.). Restaurant critics write about what they taste, then evaluate the final product of professional chefs who charge the public good money for the fruits of their labors. All restaurant critics are food writers, but rare is the food writer who is also a restaurant critic.

Most restaurant critics work on a weekly basis. (There may be critics out there who manage to eat, digest, think, and review multiple restaurants in a week, but if they exist, it's a fair bet they're either independently wealthy, really *really* fat, or crazy.) Many periodicals assign their critics to file articles on various foods and food trends in between their reviews of restaurants. In this respect, most critics, if they're good writers (more on this below), can toggle back and forth as part-time food writers. On the other hand, most cookbook authors and food writers wouldn't be caught dead writing hard-boiled opinionated prose about, for example, some phoning-it-in celebrity chef. But that's just fine with real critics, because you wouldn't want a food writer to write a proper restaurant review any more than you'd want a cheerleader to be a football coach.

In a typical week, critics will visit at least a half-dozen restaurants—most for the first time, some to get a second look—as they keep their pipelines stuffed with reviews in progress, possible subjects for future reviews, and potential food articles. Back in the Stone Age, the late 20th century, it was *de rigueur* for a critic to visit a restaurant multiple times before filing a review. These days, due to the news-a-minute immediate-gratification impact of the Internet, almost no publication, save for maybe a few major newspapers, requires critics to eat more than one meal in a restaurant before giving their opinion of it.

This is extremely unfortunate, because restaurants are not movies. Every movie critic sees the same movie; a restaurant is an organic being, dependent on the coordination of many people to do its job well. All it takes is for a dishwasher to call in sick, or a waitress to have a fight with her boyfriend, or a cook to check into rehab for you to have a lousy time. Only by eating in a place multiple times can a real critic take the measure of a place. Every place in this book has been visited multiple times by me.

Also, due to the Internet, anonymity has gone the way of the tasseled menu and the hat-check girl. All real critics writing for respected publications or wielding any real clout are known to every major restaurant in their cities. Their photos are posted in restaurant kitchens, and anyone with a mobile phone can look up anyone's picture in 30 seconds.

In the end, a restaurant writer's job description has two parts: eating and writing. The eating part isn't as easy as it seems. You have to have (or develop) an iron stomach, an adventuresome attitude, and a fine-tuned palate. You must learn to eat things you loathe and learn enough about them to objectively judge their net worth. (I'll never like beets or Vietnamese food, but I've eaten enough of both that I could start a farm or a pho parlor.)

Eating a meal (or even several) in a restaurant is no more enough to correctly opine on its merits than looking at a single painting is to judge an artist—even if you're a knowledgeable critic. To judge a steakhouse, you better have eaten in dozens of them all over the country. An amateur is one who says, "I went to Mama Leone's and really liked the lasagna." A restaurant critic has made lasagna in her home kitchen, watched professionals make it on TV, eaten lasagna in the great Italian restaurants of the world, and traveled to Bologna to see and taste the real thing. Anyone with an opinion can tell you whether something is good. I don't know beans about art, but I can tell you that that Rembrandt fellow sure looks like he knew what

Twenty Suggestions for Dining Out in Style

1. Be in a good mood. You'll get out of restaurants what you put into them. If you're looking for a slight, or a service misstep, or a flabby French fry, you'll find it. The happier you are with yourself, the less small glitches will bother you.
2. Be hungry. A surprising number of people who go out to eat aren't hungry.
3. Be in love with restaurants. What's not to love? A number of people (usually young, always attractive) are scurrying around trying to feed you and please you. A surprising number of people who go out to eat don't want to be there. Restaurants are like relationships: You must really want to be in one to make it work.
4. If you want great service in a restaurant, go there several times in a relatively short period of time. Time #1 will be pleasant enough, time #2 they'll be happy to see you again, and by time #3, you'll be treated like one of the family. When you start getting treated like one of the family, some freebie (a drink, a dessert, a taste of something special from the kitchen) usually starts showing up. By trip #3, you will also look like a total stud to whomever you're dining with.
5. Be open-minded. Restaurants aren't for picky eaters. Picky eaters should prepare their own meals at home.
6. Remember how hard it is to own or work at a restaurant. Nothing is as easy as it seems. A cook is remembering a dozen details; the dishwasher is up to his elbows in 200-degree steam; the pretty little hostess is tracking who's coming and going while she's answering the phone, seating people, and trying to keep the owner's hand off her ass.
7. Respect the staff. Be grateful they're serving you and not the other way around.
8. Look at the menu carefully. Every restaurant in the world tells

you right up front what it's good at. If there's a box at the top or bottom of the page that says: "Try our world-famous waffles!" get the friggin' waffles. *Don't* get the lasagna, fer chrissakes. If you insist on ordering a cheeseburger at place advertising wood-fired pizzas, don't say we didn't warn you.

9. Listen to the staff. Ask them what they like. Be honest with them when they ask you questions.

10. Don't ask too many questions. You're there to eat; the waiters are there to bring you food, not discuss breakthroughs in animal husbandry or the pedigree of the vegetables.

11. Be decisive. No one likes to watch you fret over the linguine versus the ravioli. Being too choosy in good restaurants is a bit like being finicky about oral sex: No matter what, you'll still enjoy yourself.

12. Only order fish in restaurants specializing in fish.

13. Order champagne right off the bat. Admittedly, this is one of my pricier pieces of advice, but if you order two glasses of expensive French champagne (or better yet, a bottle of the pricey stuff) as soon as you sit down, the wait staff will snap to your attention immediately. Works every time.

14. Unless you enjoy polluting your body with the refuse of the land and sea, avoid all-you-can-eat anything.

15. Leave your food allergies at home. Face it: You're not really allergic to anything; you just want the attention or you're fat. Or both.

16. Never order a glass of wine in cocktail bar. Never order a cocktail in a wine bar. Why do I have to keep telling you these things?

17. Show your enthusiasm. I don't care if you're in an izakaya in Tokyo, a Michelin-starred haute cuisine palace in Paris, or a lunch counter in Paducah, Kentucky, tell your waiter how happy you are to be there.

18. Dress the fuck up. If you look like a slob, you'll be treated like a slob. (Exception: barbecue restaurants. No one gives a shit how you look in a barbecue restaurant. Barbecue restaurants are the great equalizers.)

19. Never eat out on a Saturday night. Saturday night is to eating out what New Year's Eve is to drinking. Epicureans eat out on Wednesday and Thursday, when both the food and the staff are the freshest.

20. "Never eat at a place called Mom's, play cards with a man named Doc, or sleep with a woman whose troubles are worse than your own." — Nelson Algren

The Glories of Dining Alone

The Roman general Lucius Lucinius Lucullus Ponticus was one of the richest men in ancient Rome. He was known for his sumptuous banquets and feasts so elaborate (for dozens and sometimes hundreds of guests) that Pompey and Cicero refused an invitation to dine with him, fearing for the expense he'd incur for even a simple dinner.

A famous story tells of Lucullus taking his chief cook to task for a modest repast placed before the general as he dined alone. "As there were to be no guests, I thought my master would not want an expensive supper," said his chef by way of an apology.

"What?" exclaimed Lucullus. *"Dost thou not know that this evening, Lucullus dines with Lucullus?"*

If you're one of those who dreads, avoids, or maybe just hasn't mastered the art of dining alone, you're truly missing something special. Eating alone, especially in a good restaurant, is one of life's great pleasures.

I didn't always feel this way, of course. Like many of you, I used to be embarrassed to sit alone in a crowded eatery, feeling pathetic and stared-at the whole time. Rushing through the meal, I savored little and cringed a lot at my sad lonely life.

But then I saw the light.

When you make the decision (or the decision is made for you) to dine alone, look at the freedom and the unbridled hedonism that lie before you. When you dine alone:

- You can order what you want, when you want.
- There's no menu bartering with your dining companions. ("If you're having the pompano, and she's taking the salmon, I guess I'll have the sole, just for the halibut.")

- You can get as stewed as you want (as long as you're not driving).
- Table manners? Why bother?
- You can fill up on bread, or, even better, scarf down butter or olive oil with impunity. I'll admit that I enjoy shamelessly dipping a host of breads into the butter with no regard for knife or dish. Barbaric? Well, yes, but oh so satisfying.
- Red wine with fish? No problem. Three gimlets before the degustation? Why not?
- Eating salsa is so much easier. We all know how everyone has to finesse dipped chips into their mouths, avoiding the dreaded double-dip. Well, shoveling your salsa solo eliminates all that, and you don't have to share.
- You can flirt shamelessly with the hot hostesses, waitresses, or waiters, depending on who's floating your boat that evening.
- You can eat with your fingers, mix up stuff on various plates—even drink up the sauce.
- On a more serious note, you save money. The cost of a meal at gourmet destinations like Le Cirque, Savoy, or Robuchon is prohibitive. Go alone and you can concentrate on the food, discussing it in depth with the highly knowledgeable wait staffs (at least those you're not trying to pick up). Chatting up the staff becomes an education and a way to make a new friend, at a pittance of the price if two or more are present.

So, the next time you truly want to luxuriate in a great meal, try remembering that the word "luxurious" comes from the name of the noble Roman—who had no greater dining companion than when he, Lucullus, dined with himself.

Chef Worship

"He's making his own rules" is how a full-of-himself Yelper described Grant Achatz to me the other day."

"Alain Passard is a culinary god; most chefs are in awe of him."

"L'Arpège is a temple."

"Noma is a religious experience that changed everything."

"Osteria Francescana will change your life with one bite."

These days, chefs are visionaries and the rest of us merely unworthy pilgrims begging to bask in the aura of their brilliance.

Please.

We're talking about cooks here, people who take raw materials and apply heat (or not) to make them more palatable to eat. No one is curing cancer, creating masterpieces, or doing something heroic. Restaurant cooking, whether it's at a Greek diner or a Michelin-starred palace, is assembly-line cooking. It's about repetition more than creativity (there isn't a whole lot new in food and hasn't been for hundreds of years) and anyone who thinks otherwise is ... deluded. These lionized cooks have figured out a way to seduce an always-looking-for-the-next-big-thing food press that can induce the more-money-than-brains crowd to slavishly worship at the altar of some kitchen that excels in eliciting oohs and aahs from gullible customers and separating rich showoffs from their cash.

It all started when Paul Bocuse became a celebrity back in the early 1970s. "He got the chef out of the kitchen," Pierre Troisgros put it to me when I interviewed him 18 years ago. (As he uttered the words, Troigros did so with a tone of both admiration and regret. He seemed in awe of Bocuse, but also wistful for a profession he knew was changing and that he no longer understood.)

Chefs started to be a big deal in America in the '80s, but it wasn't until Tom "Call Me Thomas" Keller hit it big with the French Laundry

YELLOWTAIL SASHIMI AT RAKU

in '96-'97 that the cult of chef fetishization really took off here. Concurrent with all the hyperventilating press Keller was getting, the rise of the Food Network in the late '90s gave restaurant cooking a cachet previously reserved for rock musicians and bad-boy actors.

By 2006, every working-class kid in America suddenly had a path to being idolized as a "bad ass" or even worse, a "passionate misunderstood genius." All the while, the media, the audience, and the chefs themselves were losing sight of the big picture: Restaurant cooking is a brutally hard, endless-hours, pressure-cooker profession that, at its core, is about as glamorous as window-washing.

The rise of the interwebs and social media over the past 10 years has turned what was once annoying into the sublimely ridiculous. Every chef now has to have a following and every chef worshiper is hanging on whatever lavish food porn (e.g., the panting, hagiographic, hyper-absurd Chef's Table) or Instagrammable dish or MAJOR AWARD has been handed out that week. Cooking has thus become more about publicity and bragging rights than taste, and if there's one thing we can all agree on, it's that you can't taste publicity—or bragging rights.

Who cares if Rene Redzepi is traveling the world with a pop-up restaurant reserved for the .00001% of the people able to actually eat there? Becoming a star doesn't make anything taste any better and as soon as a chef becomes a star, he pretty much quits cooking altogether, so what, exactly, are we worshiping?

I'm pleased for any chef who can parlay his or her skills into a brand or fame or some degree of celebrity. But when it comes to what I put in my mouth, the people I worship are the ones in the kitchen, sorting the vegetables, grilling the fish, and stirring the sauce. Mexicans, mostly.

MARIO BATALI • JOE BASTIANICH
B&B

ALLEGRO (STRIP) Italian

Wynn Las Vegas
(702) 770-2040
wynnlasvegas.com
Mon.-Fri., 3 p.m.-6 a.m.; Sat.-Sun., 10 a.m.-6 a.m.
$25-$75

Since taking over the restaurant formerly known as Stratta (and as Corsa Cucina before that) three years ago, Executive Chef Enzo Febbraro has made this place sing in ways it hasn't sung since Steven Kalt left the premises in 2007. Febbraro is a Neapolitan by birth and a basso profundo by cooking temperament. Whether he's pounding a veal chop into pizza-sized impressiveness or rolling and roasting monkfish in house-made pancetta, you'll know from the first bite you're in the hands of a master.

Deep flavors are the rule here, plus a palpable sense of how to intermingle proteins with produce and build on the tastes of both with a judicious use of accents and herbs. Does anyone in town make a better Marsala? Or osso buco? Emphatically no. Neither can many Italians compete with his carpaccio or clams casino. The Food Gal (my significant other) goes crazy for his pizzas (truth be told, they're the best pies of any full-service restaurant in Vegas), and yours truly (a noted beet hater) has even been seen polishing off a plate of Febbraro's beet, bean, and pear salad. If seafood's your thing, don't miss

the calamarata, a winy stew of monkfish and lobster, or the risotto pescatora, which will knock you over with its intensity.

And we haven't even mentioned the pastas yet, the best things on the menu. If you're the sort who likes a rosemary-pepper bite with your scialatielli (and let's face it, who doesn't?), then the carbonara-tossed pasta will make you want to swim in its eggy delights. Ditto the meaty layered baked lasagna that somehow manages the feat of being hearty, rib-sticking, and delicate all at the same time.

The desserts and breads are top-notch, as is almost everything that comes out of the Wynn/Encore's bakeshop, and the wine list is well-matched to the food and not quite as bend-you-over-and-hand-the-Vaseline-oriented as some wine cards at the tonier Wynncore joints. Another plus: They stay open late, really late, 6 a.m. every morning, making this a mecca for club goers, inveterate gamblers, and the soon-to-be hung over.

GET THIS

All pastas; pizza margherita; beet and frisée salad; clams casino; carpaccio; mozzarella platter; prosciutto platter; veal Marsala; lamb osso buco; veal chop parmigiana; risotto pescatora; basically everything on the friggin' menu.

ANDRE'S BISTRO & BAR (WEST) French/American

see map 1, page 243
6115 S. Fort Apache
(702) 798-7151 / andresbistroandbar.com
Mon.-Fri., 11:30 a.m.-3:30 p.m.; Sun.-Thurs., 4:30 p.m.-9 p.m.;
Fri. & Sat., 4:30 p.m.-10 p.m.; Brunch: Sat. & Sun., 10 a.m.-3:30 p.m.
$75-$125

In the past five years, the restaurants off the Las Vegas Strip have gotten a lot better than anyone ever thought they would and André's Bistro & Bar has led this charge with a combination of a serious bar, an interesting well-priced wine list, and real French bistro food with no compromises.

This menu is all about French classics, even though they call it "American tavern cuisine." You don't get much more French than frogs and foie gras and you won't get any better seared liver than this one (it sits atop stewed apples and a caramel custard sauce). As for those frogs, their garlicky legs come along with a roasted vegetable terrine of uncommon concentrated tomato richness. Just as good are the escargot (swimming in butter, garlic, and parsley just the way they're supposed to be) and moules frites that cede no ground to anything you'll find at Bouchon, Mon Ami Gabi, or Bardot Brasserie.

Of the salads, the Lyonnaise is proper in every way and the beets with goat cheese are as beety as you could want them. No other restaurants in our neighborhoods have ever seen the top-shelf seafood risotto or a textbook-perfect Dover sole "Veronique." The house-made sausages come with some nice sweet-sour Lyonnaise potato salad (another homage to Gaul), while the nutty golden trout amandine is lightly sautéed and properly adorned with a beautiful brown butter sauce. You won't be disappointed in the flat iron steak, the frites, or the burger, either.

One place you'll want to stop and linger is the dessert menu. Tammy Alana's creations are the best thing to hit the 'burbs since free parking. Every one of them is a classics—tarte tatin, chocolate walnut gateau, milkshakes (with malt!), Grand Marnier soufflé, lemon tart—all made in-house, all tasting like you're in the hands of a master.

GET THIS

Bouillabaisse; seafood risotto; seared foie gras; frogs legs; escargot; onion soup; moules frites; housemade sausages; braised lamb shank; Dover sole Veronique; trout Amandine; Lyonnaise salad; coq au vin; duck a l'orange; flat iron steak; chocolate walnut gateau; lemon tart; root-beer float; crème brûlée.

BARDOT BRASSERIE (STRIP) French

Aria at CityCenter
(877) 230-2742
aria.com
Mon.-Fri., 5:30-10:30 p.m.; Sat. & Sun., 9:30 a.m.-10:30 p.m.
$75-$125

When Michael Mina announced he was closing American Fish at Aria and replacing it with a classic French brasserie, more than a few foodies scoffed. Didn't he know that this is the age of tiny tables, minuscule plates, insulting noise levels, and uncomfortable everything? Hadn't someone told him that traditional French style is about as hip as a dickey? And that Croque Madame and salad Niçoise were old hat by the Clinton era?

They might have told him, but we're happy he didn't listen. Instead, what he did was bring forth a drop-dead-delicious ode to the golden era of brass, glass, and béchamel-drenched sandwiches—hearty platters of wine-friendly food that many think went out of style with tasseled menus, but didn't. It just took a break for a decade.

With BB, the reasons all of these recipes became famous to begin with has come roaring back, to the delight of diners who want to be coddled and cosseted with cuisine, not challenged and annoyed. Mina had the prescience to know this, and the good sense to hire Executive Chef Josh Smith to execute his vision. Smith is an Ameri-

can through and through, but obviously has a deep feeling for this food, and every night (and via the best weekend brunch in town), he proves why classics never go out of style and overwrought, over-thought, multi-course tasting menus may soon go the way of the supercilious sommelier.

Make no mistake, Bardot Brasserie is a throwback restaurant, but a throwback that captures the heart and soul of real French food like none of its competition. It harkens to an age of comfort food from a country that pretty much invented the term. What sets it apart is the attention to detail. Classics like steak frites and quiche are clichés to be sure, but here they're done with such aplomb, you'll feel like you're on the Left Bank of Paris, only with better beef. The pâté de campagne (country house-made pâté) is a wondrous evocation of pressed pork of the richest kind, and the escargots in puff pastry show how a modern chef can update a classic without sacrificing the soul of the original recipe. The skate wing suffers not at all from being 6,000 miles from the Champs Elysée, and the lobster Thermidor—bathed in Béarnaise and brandy cream—is a glorious testament to the cuisine of Escoffier.

Most of all, though, Bardot Brasserie is an homage to the great homey restaurants of France. By going old school, Michael Mina has set a new standard in Franco-American style and made us realize what we were missing all along.

GET THIS

Lobster Thermidor; skate wing; Croque Madame; onion soup grantinée; foie gras parfait; steak tartare; duck wings à l'Orange; king crab crêpe; seared foie gras Lyonnaise; frisée aux lardons; sole meuniere; chicken roti; oak-smoked Duroc pork chop; brunch.

BAZAAR MEAT BY JOSE ANDRES (STRIP) Steakhouse

SLS Las Vegas
(702) 761-7610
slslasvegas.com
Sun.-Thurs., 5:30-10 p.m.; Fri. & Sat., 5:30-10:30 p.m.
$75-$125

José Andrés is a high priest of meat and this is his temple. Calling it a steakhouse, however, is a bit unfair, since the seafood and wacky Spanish creations (molecular olives, cotton-candy foie-gras foam, etc.) are every bit as good as the steaks. For pure carnivorous joy, I'll put Bazaar up against any porterhouse pit in the country, any day, but I'll also stake its tapas and sausage and gutsy Spanish comfort food against any this side of the Iberian Peninsula.

There's a raw bar, a ham bar, a real bar, and a bar-none selection of steaks. With all of this in mind, you will, of course, not want to miss the roasted suckling pig or the whole roasted wild turbot. That little piggy can be ordered whole in advance for a crowd of 8-10; quarter portions are available on short notice (although not usually on the menu) for smaller tables.

And if all that's not enough to distract you, the wine list may be the best Spanish card in the country.

Before you get to the big proteins, though, you'll have to navigate side one of the blackboard-sized menu. There, you'll find all sorts of temptations that will fill you up long before Porky's left leg appears. Lighter appetites should stick with fresh raw scallops, gazpacho shots, and José's Asian taco (ham, nori, topped with flying fish roe), while heartier souls will want to dive into the croquetas (stuffed with creamy ham or chicken) or the Reuben, a hollowed-out crispy mini-football of air bread upon which pastrami is draped. The super-giant light-as-a-saltine chicharron takes up half the table, but disappears quickly as it's dipped in Greek yogurt with za'tar spices, and everyone will be fighting over the last bite of patatas bravas.

One of the signs of a great steakhouse is how they treat their veggies and here, if you don't want to think about meat (difficult under the circumstances, but doable), you can splurge on stuffed piquillo peppers, Catalan spinach with raisins and pine nuts, Brussels sprouts petals with lemon purée, or a whole cauliflower steak with preserved lemon. The beefsteak tomato tartare gets the most oohs and aahs (looking like the brightest red small pizza you've ever seen), but the simple tomato salad and the endive Caesar are show-stoppers as well.

If you haven't gotten the idea by now, this is a huge menu, both sides of that big plastic board, in fact, and deciding what to eat can be somewhat daunting. The good news is they pull everything off, nightly, with the precision of a Marine Corps drill team.

When you finally get to the steaks, you'll find all the usual suspects: grain-fed, grass-fed, sirloined, flat-ironed, and skirted, but the thing to get is the "vaca vieja" eight- to ten-year-old rib steak—beef from old cows being the current fad among serious meat mavens. Aged on the hoof rather than in a locker, it competes with the best of dry-aged steaks for pure beefy minerality.

Like we said, calling this place a steakhouse is a bit of a misnomer. It's a palace of protein that even a pescatarian or a vegetarian can love. It's also one of the greatest restaurants in the world.

GET THIS

Cotton-candy foie gras; pork-skin chicharron; José's Asian taco; croquetas; Ferran Adria olives; patatas bravas; Reuben sandwich; tomato tartare; beef tartare; oysters; clams; live scallops; chef's selection of cured meats; piquillo peppers; Brussels sprouts petals; cauliflower steak; endive Caesar salad; tortilla sacromonte egg omelet with sweetbreads; grilled Galician-style octopus; roast suckling pig; whole roasted turbot; Wagyu beef cheeks; flat-iron steak; "vaca vieja" rib steak.

B&B RISTORANTE (STRIP) Italian

Venetian
(702) 266-9977
bandbristorante.com
5-11 p.m., daily
$75-$125

Our best pasta palace, B&B specializes in noodle dishes you've never heard of made with ingredients you didn't know existed. It tells the pasta, the whole pasta, and nothing but the pasta, except when it's about the sweet juicy pork chop with plumcots, or the grilled quail with charred corn, or the goat cheese torta with stone-fruit conserves. About the time when you can't decide between the spicy two-minute calamari and the chicken alla cacciatore, you turn the page, which is filled with sweet-onion mezzalunes and Alberto's pyramids "Passato." Even something as conventional as thin spaghettini gets a copious sprinkling of bottarga (cured fish roe), while beef-cheek ravioli is stuffed with crushed duck liver. There's a pasta tasting menu if you can't make up your mind (and making up your mind will be hard to do) and a seasonal tasting menu that's a bit more protein-packed.

B&B is like an old friend you visit occasionally, but who always has something new and entertaining to tell you. If you want to go the traditional route, you can stick with the classics: house-cured salumi, grilled octopus, orecchiette with sausage and rapini, steak tagliata with aceto Manodori, and flawless cannoli, and die a happy man. Or you can venture into fried zucchini with Calabrian aioli, summer-squash ravioli with herbs, pork trotter ravioli, and rabbit porchetta with a real pepperonata kick. The gnocchi with pesto Genovese will probably be the best you've ever had this side of the Cinque Terre and you'll brag about the warm lamb's tongue or fried lamb's neck once you return to your boring old fettucine Alfredo existence.

Since taking over a couple of years ago, chef Brett Uniss has made this menu sing. They try hard to do the whole locavore-thing here (within the bounds of being a high-volume Strip big-hitter located in the middle of the Mojave Desert), and props to Joe Bastianich, Mario Batali, and Executive Chef Nicole Brisson for being forerunners of this movement in Las Vegas. I used to think of B&B as a poor relation to Carnevino (its bigger bolder sibling down the hall); now I consider them equals in the knock-your-socks-off Italian food derby. The bar and cocktails are stellar as well, as is the wine list … as long as you ignore its prices.

GET THIS

Pasta, pasta, pasta; warm lamb's tongue with mixed mushrooms; lamb neck fritti; grilled quail; bavette cacio e pepe; pork trotter ravioli gnocchi with pesto Genovese; chicken cacciatore; pork chop with pluots; summer-squash ravioli; spaghettini with bottarga; goat cheese torta; rabbit porchetta; veal chop; charred sweet corn (in season); zucchini fritti; lacinato kale with smoked pork; cannoli; apricot crostada; vanilla panna cotta; cheese; and did we mention the pastas?

BLUE RIBBON (STRIP) American

Cosmopolitan
(702) 698-7880 / (702) 736-0808
cosmopolitanlasvegas.com
Sun.-Thurs., 5 p.m.-midnight; Fri. & Sat., 5 p.m.-2 a.m.
$75-$125

When Bruce and Eric Bromberg shuttered Blue Ribbon last year (after six years at the Cosmopolitan), few shed a tear for its demise. It was an attractive, if disjointed, restaurant that always seemed in the throes of an identity crisis. Was it a lounge? A sushi bar? Two different sushi bars? Who knew or cared? By trying to combine their two iconic New York City restaurants (their gutsy American bistro of the same name and the separate Blue Ribbon Fish), the Brombergs achieved the confusing result of making the whole less than the sum of its parts.

Now they've re-opened, ditched the fish, and gotten back to what they do best—cooking the most ethereal, eclectic, American comfort food on the planet. Blue Ribbon started 25 years ago in lower Manhattan. It practically invented the whole upscale American food thing (popularizing everything from bone marrow to fried catfish) and was known for the best burger in the business until Daniel Boulud came along with his foie-gras-stuffed version and got everyone on the burger bandwagon. Elevating simple food has always been the mission statement here and artistic cooking for unfussy gourmands has made BR a critic's (and chef's) darling since Bill Clinton was president. Now, with its reboot, BR has gotten back to basics. The dark loungey bar has been replaced with a bright front-and-center friendly one and the menu has returned to where it's supposed to be: chock full of the specialties that made the Brombergs famous.

No one disdains something-for-everyone menus more than yours truly, but in these hands, you can just close your eyes and point. Matzoh-ball soup? They've got you covered. Fried oysters? Leeks vinaigrette? You won't find better versions anywhere on Las Vegas Boulevard. Duroc pork ribs come sweetly glazed with their own mini-hibachi, the clam soup would make a Mainer proud, and the country pâté deserves to be in the charcuterie hall of fame. The red (sea) trout with spätzle is also a thing of beauty and the burger every bit as good as it was in 1993.

For dessert, don't miss the chocolate-chip bread pudding. It's a gut buster of the most delicious kind and easily sates four sweet tooths.

American bistro cooking is everywhere these days, but the Brombergs did it first and they still do it better than anyone. Certain restaurants that just belong in Las Vegas and the new Blue Ribbon, which is really the old Blue Ribbon, is one of them.

GET THIS

Country pâte; steak tartare; shellfish platter; bone marrow; pu-pu platter; burger; matzoh-ball soup; clam soup; leeks vinaigrette; fried oysters; Duroc pork ribs; sea trout with spätzle; fried catfish; skate with brown butter; hanger steak; fried chicken; paella Basquez; chocolate-chip bread pudding.

BOTECO (EAST)

Global Fusion

see map 3, page 245
9500 S. Eastern Avenue, #170
(702) 790-2323
botecolv.com
Tues.-Sat., 5 p.m.-11 p.m.; Sun., 10 a.m.-5 p.m.
$25-$75

When Standard & Poor closed, my (already low) opinion of the Green Valley area of Henderson plunged even further. For years I've called GV "the land of $400,000 homes and $40,000 cars where no one wants to spend more than $40 on dinner."

Just weeks before S&P shuttered, the little jewel box Boteco opened in a giant strip mall that houses at least two dozen other (mostly terrible-yet-thriving) food options. Boteco is so small and obscure—wedged between something called the Beach Hut Deli and a pet food store—that you can be parked right in front of it and miss it. But find it you should, if you want to taste Spanish-styled, chef-driven, Robuchon-inspired food the likes of which this backwater probably can't appreciate.

But you, sophisticated peruser of Las Vegas' only restaurant guidebook, will appreciate it. Since you're reading this review, you're obviously in search of good taste, and tastes don't get much better than what chef Rachel LeGloahec is putting on these plates. It isn't complicated food, a la Sparrow + Wolf, nor is it the sort of too-hip-for-the-room cooking that goes over in Henderson like a Muslim cleric at an NRA convention. These are the musings of a confident young chef who has obviously been well-trained and who hits her marks with every step.

Take her weekend brunch. Everyone knows I hate brunch. And I hate it because most brunch menus are about as inspiring as a Mitch McConnell press conference. LeGloahec got me interested from the first bite of her house-vodka-cured salmon and spiced things up with Tacos da Moda—scrambled eggs with strips of steak and Spanish chorizo ready to be rolled into some house-made corn tortillas—as beautiful a breakfast concoction as can be constructed. You'll also love the Dutch Baby-style pancakes, served with a strawberry coulis and champagne zabaglione, and their dense half-pancake/half-popover feel. The trio of Botequito sliders dripping with melted onions and smoked Gouda on a brioche bun is a burger wonder unto itself and if that's not enough to get you out of your brunch rut, the trio of prosecco "flights"—bellini, cassis, and limoncello—is a lip-smacking steal at $12.

At dinner, only 12 choices make up the menu, but those sliders, an avocado crunch salad, and a Singapore chili-crab dip are all delights, the kind of food that's unknown this far from the Strip. There's even a poutine on the menu for the calorie-challenged, fabulous Spanish ham, good oysters, and escargot croquetas and braised beef with Piedmontese rice for ectomorphs in need of a good rib-sticking. This is a mix-and-match menu that's made for fun.

Boteco means "meeting place" for friends and family, and if you and yours are looking for a place to congregate, you won't find any better in this neck of the culinary desert.

GET THIS

Botequito sliders; avocado crunch salad; Singapore chili crab; vodka-cured salmon; Tacos da Moda; escargot croquetas; braised beef with Piedmontese rice; Iberico ham; brunch; oysters; poutine; prosecco flight.

BOUCHON (STRIP) French

Venetian
(702) 414-6200
venetian.com
5-10 p.m., daily; Mon.-Thurs., 7 a.m.-1 p.m.; Fri.-Sun., 7 a.m.-2 p.m.
Oyster bar 3-10 p.m., daily
$25-$75

Thomas Keller took some pretty big hits this year. Per Se's demotion to two stars in the *New York Times* had the Internet (and *schadenfreude*-obsessed food press) all atwitter about his possibly losing his fastball. He might not be the pitcher he once was back there in Yankee Stadium, but out here in the hustings, his control is as pinpoint as ever. The epi baguettes can still blow you away from the first bite and they, like everything else on this menu, are major league. You won't find better oysters or mussels this far from an ocean and the room is just as vibrant and comfortable as it was when it opened 13 years ago.

I've eaten here dozens of times over those years and the food—whether a special silken corn soup or voluptuous veal porterhouse—never fails to astonish with its technical perfection and intensity. The wine list, like most in Gouge the Greenhorn Gulch, sticks it to you without lubrication. On the bright side, there's a nice selection of half bottles that bend you over for half the insanely inflated price. Stick with whites and light reds (think Beaujolais and vin du pays) to avoid feeling quite so violated. Those quibbles aside, asking me to choose between Bouchon and Bardot Brasserie for casual French supremacy is like asking me which one of my kids I love the most.

GET THIS

Oysters; soupe a l'oignon; corn soup (seasonal); steak frites; parfait du foie gras; moules au safran; poulet roti; truite amandine; Croque Madame; escargot; salade Lyonnaise; veal chop; boudin blanc; crème brûlée; bouchons.

CARBONE (STRIP) Italian

Aria at CityCenter
(877) 230-2742
aria.com
5:30-10:30 p.m., daily
$75-$125

Alan Richman, in reviewing the original Carbone in New York City three years ago, pointed out that all Italian-American restaurants are past their prime. He compared them with Al Pacino at the end of *Godfather III*: desiccated, dissipated, and haunted by the memories of better days. Mario Carbone and Rich Torrisi are trying to single-handedly buck this trend and resuscitate the genre by presenting an upscale, very expensive, and theatrical Italian-American joint with excellent Eye-talian food in large portions at jaw-dropping prices. If the hordes packing this place every night are any indication, by and large they're succeeding.

Carbone Las Vegas opened late last year with its New York pedigree intact and from the get-go, a reservation has been almost impossible to get. That reputation draws them in by making everyone feel as if they're in an old-school movie while they're eating there. The groovy '60s' sound track plays just the right mix of crooners and doo-wop and the atmosphere, from the tuxedoed waiters to the flaming tableside preparations, is a throwback in all the best ways. Our suggestion is to go with a crowd, go light on the booze, and be ready to do a lot of family-style noshing. That way you'll spread the cost around and try lots of dishes that would overwhelm a two-top.

Like what? Like duck-fat fried potatoes Louie, so rich they should have their own tax bracket, or very spicy rigatoni in vodka sauce that's easily enough for four to share. The $50 veal parmigiana caused quite a stir when it debuted back in the Big Apple in 2012; in Las Vegas, they charge $64 without so much as a tube of K-Y on the side. No one is batting an eye these days, so who am I to argue? Nowhere is Vegas' status as the most expensive dining city in America confirmed more than by looking at Carbone's prices.

As for wine, it's a very good Italian list, one of the best in the city, though it's best approached with your accountant in tow and a second mortgage. On the plus side, the sommeliers are super nice and very good looking.

Like the prices, everything about Carbone is over the top. Which makes it perfect for Vegas.

GET THIS

Meatballs (not on the menu, you have to ask); minestrone soup; all pastas (especially rigatoni in vodka sauce); veal parmigiana; pork chop with peppers; flaming bananas.

CARNEVINO (STRIP)

Steakhouse

Palazzo
(702) 789-4141
carnevino.com
5-11 p.m., daily
Taverna: noon-midnight
$75-$125

Carnevino isn't just one of the best steakhouses in Las Vegas; it might be the best steakhouse in the country. It's also, on any given night, one of the best Italian restaurants in America. Throw in a killer cocktail program, a spacious and inviting lounge, a world-class wine list, plus a little dynamo named Nicole Brisson—who makes the whole thing run like a fine-tuned watch—and you have a one-of-a-kind only-in-Vegas experience that deserves to be a lot more famous than it is. If Brisson were doing this kind of work in New York or Los Angeles, she would've graced numerous magazines and television shows by now.

As it is, Carnevino exists in a world of its own, a sui generis blend of superior Italian food and the country's best beef. Its "riserva" steaks are justifiably famous and you have to call ahead to reserve one that's been aged anywhere from 60 to 150 days—what Brisson considers the "sweet spot." Do so and you'll taste beef like you've never encountered it before. They're not for everyone (and the regular dry-aged ribeye and strip are otherworldly in their own right), but if you have the coin and the palate, you'll pay for the privilege of eating the most intensely gamey steaks in the world.

If beef ain't your bag, take heart. The pastas, antipasti, and fish will more than satisfy your craving for a taste of Italia. Thus does this kitchen also dazzle with everything from house-cured salumi, such as coppa, lardo, and lonza, to a variety of pastas as diverse as corn agnolotti, lobster agnolini, and linguine with crab, jalapeños, and cipollini. Put these together with an abundance of locally sourced products and you have that rarest of creatures: a huge celebrity-chef-driven Las Vegas restaurant that's also very much a part of the local food community

GET THIS

Riserva steaks; dry-aged bone-in ribeye; New York strip; lamb chops "Scottadita"; all house-cured salumi; carne crudo alla Piedmontese (steak tartare); house-cured pastrami; grilled octopus; shrimp alla diavolo; linguine with crab and jalapeños; bucatina all'amatriciana; ricotta and egg ravioli; grilled sweetbreads; veal chop; osso buco alla milanese; all pastas.

CARSON KITCHEN (DOWNTOWN) American

see map 1, page 243
124 S. Sixth Street
(702) 473-9523
carsonkitchen.com
Sun.-Wed., 11:30 a.m.-10 p.m.; Thurs.-Sat., 11:30 a.m.-11 p.m.
$25-$75

Downtown Las Vegas continues to exhibit the schizophrenia of a town founded by Mormons that makes its living off drinking, gambling, and whoring. After 112 years, it still doesn't know whether it wants to be a collection of low-rent cheap-ass casinos or a place in which people might actually want to live and hang out. The nickel-beer crowd still flocks to that gawdawful awning over the old Fremont Street; younger hipper folks (who look at slot machines the way Brigham Young did monogamy) eschew the buskers, beggars, and bunco artists for the cooler confines (as in more au courant) of East Fremont and its surrounding blocks.

Meanwhile, there's almost nothing good to eat in the downtown hotels, but Carson Kitchen dishes up a great plate of grub, as well as some hope for the future. The only problem with CK is its size. Seating only 40, it fills up quickly. And when it's full, it's loud. Too loud for Boomers of a certain age, but just what Gen-Xers and Millennials seem to find appealing. Personally, I ignore the amplitude and concentrate on the amplifood. Because whatever you get will ring your chimes to go along with that ringing in your ears.

The menu is small but mighty and there's not a clunker on it. The communal "social plates" always get you started on the right foot: Crispy chicken skins come with smoked honey and gyro tacos get stuffed with lamb and tzatziki. They compete with barbecue burnt ends slathered in sauce and veal meatballs coated with sherry-foie gras cream. The bacon jam with baked brie is no slouch either and the sour-sweet artichoke is a thistle that will whet your whistle. A "filet-ohhh-fish" is more like a fishcake than a filet and comes with a green goddess cole slaw, the rotating cast of flatbreads are flat-out wonderful, and the "Secret Sunday Chicken" puts Chick-fil-A to shame. Sure, it costs twice as much, but it's also twice as good. The "Butter Burger," an homage to Wisconsin, is all you could want in an upscale patty and the short-rib grilled cheese (oozing with fromage) is … wait for it … gouda enough for two.

Bigger proteins, such as sea bass, strip steak, and chops, get treated with respect (and in-your-face sauces) and the "farm-and-garden" options are, simply stated, wonderful.

They rotate things seasonally here, but the baked mac and cheese is always present, as are the mega-rich black rice with oxtail risotto and the spicy shrimp and grits. In summer, don't miss the watermelon and feta, and whenever they're on the menu, close your eyes and order whatever this kitchen is doing with Brussels sprouts, broccoli, or cauliflower.

Simplicity is the secret to CK's success. If you eat there a lot, as I do, you notice the straightforward recipes and direct flavors. The reach of this kitchen never exceeds its grasp, even as it constantly stretches for excellence. In some ways, the food is like the room: boisterous and a little too small for its ambitions. Downtown denizens wouldn't have it any other way.

GET THIS

Crispy chicken skins; bacon jam with brie; tempura green beans; gyro tacos; veal meatballs; BBQ burnt ends; devil's eggs; grilled artichoke; butter burger; filet-ohhh-fish; secret Sunday chicken sandwich; pork chop; sea bass; flatbreads; shrimp & grits; watermelon and feta; black rice and oxtail risotto; bourbon fudge brownie; glazed-donut bread pudding.

CHADA STREET/CHADA THAI & WINE (WEST) Thai

see map 1, page 243
3839 Spring Mtn. Road / 3400 S. Jones Boulevard
(702) 579-0207 / (702) 641-1345
chadastreet.com / chadavegas.com
Tues.-Sun., 5 p.m.-3 a.m.
$25-$75

Chada Street has a big sign announcing its presence, a mile west of the Strip in a large almost all-Asian strip mall right on Spring Mountain Road. Chada Thai is tucked into a small all-Asian strip mall a couple of miles farther west. Chada Street you can't miss; Chada Thai you can miss standing right in front of it.

Both are relatively small with excellent service, neither is open for lunch (tragic), and oenophiles will like both (minimal markups). Chada Street is brighter and more casual. Large groups will do better at Street; first dates will be impressed by Thai. Street aims for rougher, urban, spicier fare, befitting its moniker, while Thai skews more toward traditional regional dishes, albeit with much nicer presentations, and in a more sophisticated setting than your usual neighborhood joint.

Look for dishes labeled "medium spicy" at both if you want to enjoy what you're eating; it enables you to enjoy both the food and those delicious white wines that complement it. Anyone who doesn't like the electric jolt of Thai chilies should book elsewhere.

The food at both is superb. At Thai, chef Bon Atcharawan is as

adept with crispy deep-fried oysters and larb as he is with sea bass. Tilapia is on the menu in various guises, but the sea bass is the swimmer to get. Just as essential on this menu are the miang pou (crab-stuffed lettuce wraps), almost raw ribeye (yum nua) marinating in chili-lime dressing, green papaya salad (som thum), the house-made beef jerky (nua dad diew), and the rice-powder-dusted crispy beef (pla nua tod), a study in crunchy spicy beefiness.

One of the reasons for the enduring popularity of Thai cuisine is it never gets boring. These recipes have been honed over a millennium to orchestrate a controlled riot of flavors. (Mediocre Thai restaurants always overplay the gloppy sweet-meets-heat paradigm and miss the herbaceous sour-bitter subtlety that characterizes a finer hand in the kitchen.)

From top to bottom, the kitchen at Chada Thai seems to ace dish after dish effortlessly. A small but mightier restaurant you will not find in Las Vegas.

No matter what your savory compulsions, you won't want to miss the Thai toast or the mango with sticky rice (in season) at either location. No matter how you slice your vertical bread, what Atcharawan and Wanmaneesiri are doing at these two restaurants is phenomenal. Having these two mega-hot Thais in town is one of the coolest things about eating and drinking in Las Vegas.

GET THIS

Chada Street: Yum hoi (blanched oysters with lemongrass); peak kai saap (spicy chicken wings); larb moo (ground pork with chili); koi nua (raw diced filet mignon); sai oua (northern Thai spicy sausage); tom yum nam (spicy and sour shrimp soup); duck Panang (duck curry); kao pad mun pu (crab-fat fried rice); moo tod nam pla (marinated pork belly); ka moo tod (crispy pork hock); Rieslings; Gewurtztraminers; gruner veltliners; and Champagnes that go with this food like flames and a fire hose.

Chada Thai & Wine: Miang pou (lettuce wrap with crab); kua kling (ground pork with house curry paste); pou nim pad prik thai (stir-fried soft-shell crab); larb; yum nua (ribeye steak with chili paste-lime dressing; fried oyster; lo-ba (fried pigs ears, tongue, heart); hoi jor (deep-fried pork roll); drunken noodle; sea bass tod krueng; pla nua tod (crispy beef with rice powder).

CHENGDU TASTE (WEST) Chinese

see map 1, page 243
3950 Schiff Drive
(702) 437-7888
11 a.m.-3 p.m., 5-10 p.m.; daily
$25 or less

From the moment it opened, Chengdu Taste was packed. Which tells you something about the power of social media these days, and how quickly word travels when an offshoot of one of L.A.'s best Chinese restaurants opens in Vegas. The original in Alhambra was anointed one of SoCal's finest by Jonathon Gold, and that was all it took to get the Chinese cognoscenti lined up outside of this obscure location on Schiff Drive when it opened about a year ago.

Along with J&J Szechuan and Yunnan Garden, Chengdu forms sort of a holy trinity of tongue-numbing eating, all of them specializing in highly spiced take-no-prisoners Szechuan/Sichuan cooking. To eat this food is to feel like small jolts of electrons have been activated in your mouth and body and tucking into a heaping platter of cumin lamb or won tons swimming in chili oil is a fine introduction to its pain/pleasure conundrum.

Whether it's skewers, starches, chicken in green sauce, or dandan mian (noodles), what you're getting here is the real enchilada. There's none of that "how hot do you want it?" nonsense that Thai restaurants fool with. Here you order and hang on for dear life. The beauty of this fare is that those chilies always seem to enhance the flavor of the proteins, not overwhelm them. In those dandan mian, the chewy noodles have a flavor of their own that comes through, as do the ground pork and pickled-vegetable sauce lying in the bottom of the bowl. You appreciate the individual ingredients even as the whole is exceeding the sum of its parts. All the while your eyeballs are sweating and you can't feel your lips.

Just as revelatory is "Diced Rabbit With Younger Sister's Secret Recipe," which is as bony as it is cold and coated with a fetching fermented heat. Those bones will drive you batty, but it's a real litmus test for budding gourmands who want to see what all the Sichuan shouting is about. We generally avoid hot pots (because everything ends up tasting the same), but you'll go nuts over the boiled fish in green sauce. For twenty bucks, you can get fresh fish (most likely tile fish or tilapia) that will easily feed four adults and boasts chilies from across the spectrum of heat. Those ubiquitous peppercorns wrap around your tongue, but set off, rather than obliterate, the taste and texture of the fish.

Chengdu Taste isn't our best Chinese restaurant in the sense that the high-toned Mandarin-pitched Wing Lei is, but it is our most authentic. And its presence on Spring Mountain Road is further evidence of the excellence in our ever-expanding roster of Asian eateries.

P.S. For all of its popularity, table turnover is fairly fast and service is almost preternaturally quick. Our advice: Get there before noon or pick an early weeknight and you'll have no problems. The staff is bilingual and helpful and the menu is full of pretty pictures and easy to navigate (not always the case on Spring Mountain Road).

GET THIS

Lamb skewers with cumin; green-sauce chicken; dandan noodles; boiled fish in green sauce; shredded potato with vinegar; fried chicken with pepper; ma po tofu (tofu in chili sauce); Szechuan sautéed string bean; won ton in red chili sauce; Diced Rabbit with Younger Sister's Secret Recipe; twice-cooked pork; won ton with pepper sauce.

CHICA (STRIP) Latin

Venetian
(702) 805-8472
venetian.com
Mon.-Fri., 8 a.m.-11 p.m.; Brunch: Sat. & Sun., 10 a.m.-4 p.m.;
Dinner: Sat. & Sun., 4-11 p.m.
$25-$75

Welcome to Las Vegas, the world capital of something-for-everyone restaurants. Reading a Las Vegas menu is like being stuck in an endless loop of pasta, pizza, wings, Caesar salad, shrimp, steak, pork, chicken, and salmon. If you're lucky, you might find another fish, and if you're really lucky, you might be treated to every pork-bellied bone-marrowed cliché in the book. Every Vegas menu, at its core, is composed of the same basic appetizers, vegetables, and proteins. Only on the margins do things get interesting and it's up to the intrepid gourmand to hunt for the nuggets of deliciousness buried in the same-old same-old stew.

At the just-opened Chica, those nuggets are everywhere and you don't even have to look that hard to find them. At first glance, you might be excused for thinking that Chica's menu is a fount of clichés in its own right. Your glance quickly picks up the mandatory guacamole, tacos, calamari, quesadilla, Caesar, and ceviche that you've seen hundreds of times before. Turn to page two and you find the mandatory chicken, shrimp, steak, and fish. At first, your heart might sink, thinking it's in another by-the-numbers Mexican tourist joint.

But then you remember that Lorena Garcia (of Food Network fame) is at the guts of the operation. With that, your spirits soar and to your delight, the flights of fancy will continue on every bite coming out of this pan-Latin kitchen.

To be clear, Chica is not a Mexican restaurant. It's a "Lorena Garcia" restaurant and the Venezuelan is all about introducing you to the glories of empanadas, amarillo, choclo, and all sorts of interesting South and Central American foods and flavors. You'll get Latino cuisine here, and South American, and food that reminds you of Mexican, but that's decidedly not Mexican. And for that, all we can say is, "Praise the Lord and pass the arepas!"

Appetizers are listed as "hot" and "cold" and you'll want to load your table with several of each. The arepa basket is filling, but worth every bite, and the grilled-corn lollipops are messy, but worth every napkin. Octopus is everywhere these days (I remember when it was only in sushi bars), but you won't find a better version than this one—atop crispy quinoa and speckled with aji amarillo sauce and guasacaca pico. On the chillier side are a classic ceviche and a Caesar salad made with watercress; the former is an exercise in perfect simplicity and the latter is the best bastardization we've ever encountered. (Note to chefs: If you're going to call something a Caesar that isn't a Caesar, take a tip from these two pros and make it with watercress.)

The proteins are predictable, but the seasonings are anything but. Meyer-lemon chicken is given a chimichurri kick, rolled porchetta comes with yucca hash and a pickled-pearl-onion escabeche, and the firm juicy halibut has been marinated in achiote, then roasted in a banana leaf. The effect is subtle, but it's a great new take on an old fish. Desserts are the handiwork of Sara Steele (another Strip veteran).

It's time to spread your Latino wings and Garcia and Steele are just the right flight instructors.

GET THIS

Arepas basket; grilled corn lollipops; Peruvian octopus; mushroom quesadilla; ceviche; watercress Caesar; butter lettuce jicama salad; Meyer lemon chicken; porchetta with yucca hash; shrimp and quinoa cazuela; Yucatan halibut; mac con queso; churros; brunch.

CUT BY WOLFGANG PUCK (STRIP) Steakhouse

Palazzo
(702) 607-6300
palazzolasvegas.com / wolfgangpuck.com
5:30-11 p.m., daily
$75-$125

Every restaurant in Las Vegas would be a steakhouse if it could be and every steakhouse secretly wishes it were CUT. Steakhouses frame our eating scene like green felt outlines a casino pit, and the numbers these meat emporiums do are staggering. Except for a few slow weeks in summer, this offshoot of the original in Beverly Hills is packed nightly with happy carnivores and meat-craving conventioneers, all ready to blow a car payment on food and a house payment on wine. Having one of the best locations in the world doesn't hurt—a thousand people must walk by the front door every hour—and sourcing some of the best steaks in the business keeps the stiff competition (Morel's and Carnevino on the other side of the casino, Delmonico right around the corner) at bay and punters lined up.

CUT dazzles with its meat (corn-fed, dry-aged, or Wagyu) and everything else it does, including one of helluva cheese cart. As great as those steaks are, I like to swim through the appetizers and sides when I'm paddling around this menu. (For that matter, the seafood is no slouch and the wild-caught turbot is a must if it's on the menu the night you visit.) There's even an argument to be made that you should park yourself in the bar and partake of addictive chili-lime popcorn, duck-tongue pastrami, or the best mini-sliders you've ever had. Making a meal out of some hot gruyere-coated gougeres and Alaskan king crab rolls isn't bad idea either. (The actual bar is small and tucked in a corner, but the bar room is copious and offers all sorts of seating for sipping or full-scale noshing. In some ways, first-class people watching being one of them, we prefer it to the main dining room.)

The starters set a new standard for steakhouse perfection. Don't miss the warm veal-tongue salad, crab and shrimp Louis, and bone-marrow flan with mushroom marmalade. The maple-glazed ten-spice pork belly will ruin you for any other version (as well as that 20-ounce sirloin you just ordered), and the seasonal salads are fresh, piquant, and balanced. The sides are equally entrancing: tempura onion rings, soft polenta with Parmesan, cavatappi mac and cheese with Quebec cheddar, shaved baby squash with basil in a "bagna cauda" sauce, haricot verts (from some California artisanal angel), and woodsy wild mushrooms like you've never tasted before.

Those steaks, grilled over hardwood and broiler-finished, are as good as you'll find (Wolfgang Puck and Executive Chef Matthew Hurley get the pick of the prime), but if you need a beef break, get the Kurobuta pork chops or rack of lamb.

Desserts are the most ambitious of any steakhouse in Vegas and pastry chef Nicole Erle can whip up a chocolate soufflé with the best of them ... when she's not constructing a baked Alaska or mascarpone-stuffed baked pear.

Before the sweets, however, you must get the cheese. They've assembled a seasonal selection here that is the envy of many a French restaurant. Like everything else about CUT, it's unique and satisfying in ways you didn't think a steakhouse could be.

GET THIS

Alaskan king crab rolls; duck-tongue pastrami; crab and shrimp "Louis"; gougeres; mini-sliders; hand-cut fries; bone marrow flan; roasted turbot; Dover sole, lamb chops; maple-glazed pork belly; veal-tongue salad; dry-aged sirloin; dry-aged ribeye; American Wagyu porterhouse for two; cavatappi pasta mac & cheese; haricot vert; wild field mushrooms; tempura onion rings; cheese cart; cookies and cream baked Alaska; mascarpone-stuffed baked pear; chocolate soufflé.

DISTRICT ONE (WEST) — Asian

see map 1, page 243
3400 S. Jones Boulevard, Suite 8
(702) 413-6868
districtonelv.com
Wed.-Mon., 11 a.m.-2 a.m.
$25 or less

Chef/owner Khai Vu is standing Vietnamese food on its ear and creating glamour in a cuisine that used to have all the sex appeal of Hillary Clinton. He's doing this by staying true to the idiom of the country—food rich in fresh herbs, accents, and sour fermented flavors and loaded with contrasts in both texture and aromas—but tweaking it into small sexy plates (and big soup statements) as far from the same old same old as soft-shell crabs are from Mrs. Paul's fish sticks.

Take his Vietnamese carpaccio. Thinly pounded sirloin is stretched provocatively over a rectangular plate, then "marinated" in fresh lime juice and drizzled with sizzling sesame oil. The effect is at once familiar and strange; the oil and acid create a warm salad-like taste and the sliced onions and fried garlic all pop in your mouth with every bite.

Vu doesn't stop there when it comes to mixing his metaphors. Chinese bao (pork-belly buns) are getting as ubiquitous as cheeseburgers, but he gives his a Southeast Asian bent with lightly pickled

daikon and carrot, micro-cilantro, and fresh-roasted and crushed peanuts.

Traditional pho fans might balk, but Vu's lobster pho is worth a special trip and his yellowtail collar is worth two. Perfectly grilled, clean-tasting, soft, buttery, and succulent, it's the apotheosis of this fish, as good as any Japonaise interpretation.

Other standouts include the five-spices roasted Cornish hen and slow-braised pork belly in young coconut juice; each will have your entire table fighting for the last morsel. The groceries used here are a notch or three above District One's competitors and the cooking is more careful, more interesting, and more scrumptious than you'll find in any Vietnamese restaurant in the Mojave Desert.

We used to think all Vietnamese food tasted alike, until Khai Vu showed up on the scene to re-interpret it for us. Even better, he's opened a downtown branch—called Le Pho—where his tasty takes on banh mi, vermicelli bowls, and hoi nan chicken rice are becoming legends in their own right.

GET THIS

Lobster pho; carpaccio of beef; Hue spicy beef noodle soup; the Big Bone soup; bao pork-belly buns; five-spice roasted Cornish game hen; beef and lemongrass wrapped in betel leaves; grilled whole squid; slow-braised pork belly in coconut juice; clay-pot chicken rice.

'E' BY JOSE ANDRES (STRIP) Spanish

Cosmopolitan
(702) 698-7000
ebyjoseandres.com
Tues.-Sun., 5:30 & 8:30 p.m. seatings
$125 and up

My affection for José Andrés is inversely proportional to my dislike of molecular cuisine. Life is too short to be confused by your food and the whole culinary sleight-of-hand that was all the rage a decade ago is pretty much played out by now. But if you let your guard down, this six-year-old restaurant-within-a-restaurant (Jaleo) will win you over with passion and precision for tweezer food that turns out to be a ton of fun. By way of comparison, if you've ever endured the humorless three-hour slog that is dinner at Alinea, you know how tedious modern food can be. Here, they keep things breezing along and send home 16 diners a night with big smiles on their faces.

Once you score a reservation (done online and not as hard as it sounds, although it may take a week or two to bag a couple of seats), walk into the sanctum sanctorum and hang on tight. What you're in for are 25+ courses of the most dazzling cooking you're likely to find anywhere in America. It's a hoot of an experience, a must for any ardent foodie. It's definitely not for traditionalists, or someone who demands large proteins with his evening meal, or those who like a few carbs with their foamy this and immersion-circulated that. (There are practically none.)

What you'll also get, if you're lucky, are the sweetest clams you'll ever taste under espuma (foam), molecular olives that are still a treat (no matter how many times you've had them), and an Ibérico ham soup that is as odd and intense a broth as you'll ever experience. Man does not live by molecule manipulation alone, so expect gorgeous fish and meat courses to round out your meal and meld perfectly with the (mostly Spanish) wines chosen for the occasion.

From what we observed, the average customer for this experience is an upper-middle-class Gen-X gastronaut, for whom this sort of experience is a necessary station on the cross of their gourmet education. Aging Boomers may consider all this molecular folderol to be the equivalent of kids playing in a gastronomic sandbox, but take heart: You will still be blown away by five chefs employing every trick in the book to satisfy and sate your culinary curiosity.

GET THIS

There is no ordering, so whatever they're making is what you'll get. With any luck, you'll be served José's sangria; beet gazpacho; José's tacos; oyster and oyster; Ibérico ham soup; clams in orange espuma; Spanish pizza; morels en papillote; fluke with caviar; crema Catalana egg; ribeye beef cap; plus a dozen other eye-popping creations.

EATT GOURMET BISTRO (WEST) French

see map 2, page 244
7865 W. Sahara Avenue, Suite 104-105
(702) 608-5233
eattfood.com
Lunch: Mon.-Sat., 10:30 a.m.-5 p.m.; Sun., 10:30 a.m.-4 p.m.
Dinner: Mon.-Thurs., 5 p.m.-8:30 p.m.; Fri. & Sat., 5 p.m.-9:30 p.m.
$25-$75

When Eatt Gourmet Bistro opened its doors a year ago, I was less than confident in its chances for success. The location on West Sahara had been the graveyard of a number of places, ranging from health food to barbecue, and the name it began with (Eatt Healthy Food) inspired neither optimism nor appetite.

What the place had in spades, though, was the faith of its owners. The three of them (chefs Yuri Szarzeweski and Vincent Pellerin, along with manager Nicolas Kalpokdjian) exuded the confidence of youngsters who didn't know what they were getting into.

Szarzweski and Pellerin trained with some of the best chefs in France and their technical proficiency is impressive, including some pretty high-flying recipes. On the other hand, I'm concerned that they're perhaps too good for the 'burbs; it's well-known that most Las Vegans favor familiar food at bargain prices, and familiar this food is not.

There's nothing ordinary about gorgeous cantaloupe "roses" accented with balsamic crisps or octopi carpaccio of uncommon

awesomeness. Medallions of glazed pork in a pea purée are a tough sell off the Strip. The neighborhoods of Las Vegas have never seen anything like a supple duck breast atop a silky corn purée dotted with fresh blueberries, baby corn, and popcorn—a dish that sounds a bit odd, looks a bit strange, and tastes a bit more than wonderful.

Seasonal eating is something to which most neighborhood joints only give lip service. At Eatt, you get not one seasonable soup, but two: a cold asparagus and a gazpacho in summer, both so vibrant with veggies you're tempted to order a second bowl and forget about the rest of your meal altogether. The seasonal vibe carries through the entire menu, from the martini glass of king crab to the beautifully composed burrata with cubed tomatoes and pesto. As for Pellerin's desserts, top to bottom, they're just about perfect.

This is sophisticated food to be sure, the most refined cooking by far anywhere outside of a major hotel. In many ways, it reminds me of a more casual, slightly less refined version of Twist by Pierre Gagnaire.

Clean, precise, inventive French food, on West Sahara at Buffalo. Who would've thunk it five years ago?

GET THIS

Cold asparagus soup; goat-cheese tartine; octopus carpaccio; salmon and tuna ceviche; beet salad; king crab cocktail; ratatouille; burrata with pesto; cantaloupe with balsamic crisps; pork with pea purée; duck breast with blueberries; whatever is in season; whatever Vincent Pellerin is cooking up for dessert.

ELIA AUTHENTIC GREEK TAVERNA (WEST) Greek

see map 2, page 244
4226 S. Durango Drive
(702) 284-5599
elialv.com
Mon.-Sat., 11:30 a.m.-10 p.m.; Sun., noon-9 p.m.
$25-$75

Is there anyone who doesn't take false advertising by restaurants for granted? How many times have you just shrugged when you saw "homemade" on a menu or "Voted Best" on a sign? So inured are we to the hyperbole of food puffery that we barely blink when something tells us that some foodstuff is the greatest this, the most authentic that, or the healthiest the other. Most of the time, most of us presume the exact opposite of what's being touted and no one bats an eyelash.

When it comes to "authentic" Greek food, as Elia claims in its name, most Greek restaurants are co-conspirators against consumers and the land of their birth. Like the Chinese and Italians before them, these immigrants created facsimiles of recipes that dumbed down the real thing. Why? Why else? Because, they thought, and rightly at the time, Americans couldn't handle the truth.

However, unlike other ethnic restaurateurs who simply watered things down, Greeks have invited entire countries into their kitchens. Thus, you can often find everything from mezze platters (Persia) and falafel (Syria) to hummus (Israel), Caesar salads (America), and kebabs (Turkey) in your average Greek restaurant. Imagine French chefs cooking up a passel of pizza, bratwurst, and bangers in a bistro and you'll get the idea. The bastardization of the real food started decades ago and it shows no signs of abating, as most Greek now gets compromised by a lava flow of babaganoush and enough shingles of pita bread (Lebanon) to tile a roof.

Amidst our raging Aegean Sea of mediocrity is an island of Hellenic serenity. With nary a cliché in sight, Elia Authentic Greek Taverna opened its doors recently and immediately started changing people's preconceptions about this cuisine. No Greek flags fly. No hideous Greek statuary adorns. The color scheme is not another variation of bright blue and white. The walls are muted, the linens are thick, and the tablecloths are real cotton. Even the bouzouki music is tuned to a nice conversational level. In short, this small 30-seat space is unlike any American-Greek restaurant you have ever been to.

Small it may be, but mighty are what come out of this kitchen. Whole fish, supple grilled octopus, gorgeous oregano-dusted lamb chops, oven-roasted lemon potatoes, superb tomato salad, gigante beans, and the big four of savory dips (tzatziki, tarama, tyrokafteri, and skordalia) all pay homage to the kind of food that Greeks themselves take for granted at home or in the neighborhood taverna. The all-Greek wine list is well-priced and the welcome makes you feel like you belong—because you do and because real Greek food finally does in America. The only untrue thing about Elia is that it's not located on a side street in Athens.

GET THIS

Greek salad; dolmades (stuffed grape leaves); kolokythakia (fried zucchini); savory dips (skordalia, tyrokafteri, tarama, tzatziki); pork gyro sandwich; gigante beans; grilled octopus; spanokopita (spinach and cheese pie); meatballs; roasted feta cheese; lamb chops; Greek potatoes; whole fish; souvlaki; Greek hamburger; galataboureko (semolina custard in phyllo).

ESTIATORIO MILOS (STRIP) Greek

Cosmopolitan
(702) 698-7000
cosmopolitanlasvegas.com
Lunch: 11 a.m.-3 p.m., daily;
Dinner: Sun.-Thurs., 5-11 p.m.; Fri.-Sat., 5 p.m.-midnight
$75-$125

The fresh fish selection here is as stunning as the bill you'll receive for it, but don't let that deter you. What's on your plate will cost a pretty penny, but that's only because you're paying for these Aquarians to taste as fresh as they did when they were lifted from the Mediterranean Sea less than a day before.

Everyone starts with the Milos special, a fried tower of zucchini chips with tzatziki and fried cheese, but you can't go wrong with the crudo (raw fish), tomato and feta salad, or any of those creamy or earthy dips (taramosalata, skordalia) that the Greeks do better than anyone. They've given up trying to teach people to say avgotaraho, and list this cured mullet roe under its more familiar Italian name: bottarga. No matter what you call it, the Greek version beats any you'll find in any Italian restaurant on these shores. When fresh Portuguese sardines are available, you should get them, and when you see the bright red Carabinieros shrimp, you should suck some sherry out of their decapitated heads like good Greeks and Spaniards do. They're not cheap, but the experience—again, costly though it is—is memorable, tasting like the richest lobster bisque you've ever had.

It's easy to go on about the fish here and what I'm raving about might not be available when you visit, but whatever is will be impeccable, grilled whole, de-boned, and served in the simplest of ways. Greek fishermen think a sprig of seasoning and a squeeze of lemon is all a great fish needs to show its best and that philosophy informs this menu. That said, an entire milokopi, encased and baked in a salt crust, is a mighty impressive way to lock in the flavor of these sublime swimmers.

Landlubbers won't be disappointed in the superb steaks and lamb chops off these grills and vegetarians will have no trouble chowing down on the plant matter they season and treat with respect.

Greek wines fit this food like feta cheese and phyllo and the list here is impressive and (relatively) affordable. Don't even try to pronounce them, just ask the expert sommeliers for guidance and a language lesson.

No mention of Milos is complete without a plug for the $30 three-course lunch. It's by far the best way to experience this cuisine without breaking the bank and it's proved so popular that reservations, or an early arrival, are mandatory if you want to snare a seat.

About the only thing I don't like about Milos are the desserts. There's nothing wrong with them (yogurt and fruits, baklava, and the like), they're just boring, even by Greek standards.

GET THIS

Carabinieros shrimp; crudo Greek tomato salad; Milos special; Maryland crab cake; sardines; grilled octopus; taramosalata dip; avgotaraho (bottarga); Milokopi fish in salt crust; fresh whole fish; lavraki (Mediterranean sea bass); fried barbounia (red mullet); Dover sole; Greek potatoes; grilled vegetables; herb couscous; lunch special.

FERRARO'S ITALIAN RESTAURANT (EAST) Italian

see map 1, page 243
4480 Paradise Road
(702) 364-5300
ferraroslasvegas.com
Mon.-Fri., 11:30 a.m.-2 a.m.; Sat.-Sun., 4 p.m.-2 a.m.
$75-$125

I've eaten at Ferraro's more times than I can count. I ate here in its pre-great-wine-list phase, its "the-only-good-Italian-restaurant-in-town" phase, its pink-neon phase, and its "let's-move-closer-to-the-Strip" phase. I've seen Ferraro's through so many phases, you'd think it was one of my unruly children. Sometimes it's felt like one.

For 32 years I've loved this place, but I haven't always been in love with it. These days, I *am* in love with it. That's because, a couple of years ago, an Italian Renaissance of the most delicious kind took place on Paradise Road. That was when the Ferraro family—Calabrians by birth and temperament (i.e., fiery)—had the good sense to put a Sicilian (no shrinking violets themselves) in charge of the kitchen. Francesco di Caudio thus turned a restaurant that's been good for decades into one that's great, by bringing some southern swagger and attention to detail to the kitchen. Di Caudo prepares sausages in house, cooks an Apulian burrata with mushrooms to die for, serves trippa satriano that makes the family proud, and does things with tagliarni with Castelmagno cheese that would put a Milanese into a swoon. Everyone gets the osso buco (and it's

great), but the coniglio brasato (braised rabbit with soft polenta) is the dish to try. The pasta dishes are full of swagger and even the simple cacio e pepper spaghetti will have you wondering if noodles can taste any better.

Ferraro's has always had a good wine list. About a dozen years ago, it started having a great one. Now, it has a *lista dei vini* that might be one of the best Italian lists in the country. Even better is the fact that paterfamilias Gino loves to discount amazing obscure bottles of serious wine to keep his inventory moving. (If you want to quibble with the wine program, you might wish the by-the-glass offerings were a bit more inventive.)

But quibbles will quickly be quashed after one bite of di Caudo's sardines, or his silky-smooth tomato risotto, or a calf's liver in red wine that will make you weep. Whatever phase this one turns out to be, I hope it stays in place for a long while.

GET THIS

Trippa satriano; tortellini; osso buco; gnocchi pomodoro; polpettine (meatballs); Apulian burrata with mushrooms and artichoke; carpaccio; house-made sausage; spaghettini aglio e olio; manzo tonnato; risotto; braised rabbit; pappardelle mimmo; tiramisu; lots and lots of red wine.

HIROYOSHI JAPANESE CUISINE (WEST) Japanese

see map 1, page 243
5900 W. Charleston Boulevard, #10
(702) 823-2110
hiroyoshi702.com
Tues.-Sun., 5-9:30 p.m.; Thurs. & Fri., 11:30 a.m.-2 p.m.
$25-$75

The latest in our wave of Edomae sushi restaurants is, by far, the farthest from the economic eating engine that is Spring Mountain Road. By several miles, in fact. Hiroyoshi is in such an obscure place for a restaurant of its quality that you have to question the sanity of one Hiro Yoshi, a former sushi chef at Blue Ribbon, for taking over the space to begin with. But any doubts you have as to his state of mind will evaporate the moment after you take your first bite. Bear in mind, this is Tokyo-style sushi. The real deal. Fine fish, finely cut, and served on rice so pure, you can count the grains in your mouth.

Don't even bother to show up if you're the sort who eschews fresh fish for overwrought inside-out sushi rolls. Being no fool, Hiro-san includes some specialty rolls on his menu (unlike Yui and Kabuto), so here you can get a Dragon Maki Mega Roll, if that's your bag. But the reason to seek out this place is Hiro-san's knife work, and to eat impeccable fresh fish on even more impeccably seasoned rice. Or to enjoy an umami-bomb of grilled cod with mushrooms or unagi (eel), stuffed tamago (egg), or the drop-your-chopsticks intricate sashimi plate. For the truly adventurous among you are also gelati-

nous strands of jellyfish, containing more texture than taste, which will bolster your street cred among the "bizarre-foods" crowd. All of it is part of an $85/pp omakase that stands up to anything Yui or Kabuto can throw at you and puts most sushi on the Strip to shame.

Put it all together and you have a neighborhood sushi bar that feels like it relocated from Shibuya. The fact that it exists at all, and seems to be thriving, is a testament to how far our Japanese eating has come.

About the only thing to criticize is the size of the (very limited) sake list. But in a 30-seat restaurant, there's only so much room for storage. Just like in the teeny tiny sushi bars of Tokyo.

GET THIS

Chef's omakase; sashimi plate; tempura platter.

JALEO (STRIP) Spanish

Cosmopolitan
(702) 698-7950
jaleo.com
Lunch: noon-4 p.m., daily;
Dinner: Sun.-Thurs., 4-11 p.m.; Fri.-Sat., 4 p.m.- midnight
$75-$125

The paella pit alone is worth the price of admission. On it lies a rectangular grill fronted by several small bonfires that blaze away underneath pans the size of manhole covers. In these pans are the purest smokiest expression of Spain's most iconic one-dish meal. If you're the sort who gets excited by these things, you can stand and watch the flames lap up the sides of steel loaded with various proteins and veggies on their way to becoming the best paella in America.

You can sit at the highboy tables beside the pit or at the cocktail bar. Or hunker down in the large low-ceiling room at one of the low-slung banquettes and pick from a variety of gin and tonics, practically the Spanish national cocktail. Wherever you sit, you'll be treated to the ongoing action of the fires and cacophony of a tapas bar that never misses a beat. The room mimics the vibe of the original in Washington D.C., but presents as a big Vegas joint that hasn't lost its original point of view, a perspective that embraces the foods of Spain, both traditional and modern.

This attitude is informed by the force of nature of its celebrity chef, José Andrés. Andrés doesn't so much cook as he inspires, cheerleads, and imbues ThinkFoodGroup (the corporation behind him) with a passion for quality that most other celebrity-chef outlets never approach.

It's impossible to get bored with Andrés' food. The menu is so varied and the quality is so high that pointing and picking are half the fun. If there's a first among equals in the tapas, it's the tomato bread—crusty rough slices on which fresh tomatoes have been grated into a pulverized mass of sweet flesh and juice. It's the simplest sounding thing in the world, but when done right as it's done here, it will send your palate into spasms of satisfaction. The same bread contributes to the best tuna-salad sandwich you've probably ever eaten and you won't find a better goat-cheese salad or gambas al ajillo, shrimp with garlic, on any $25 (for three courses) lunch menu anywhere. No one makes a better gazpacho or patatas bravas, and the hanger steak is the envy of many a steakhouse.

I like to come at lunch when the douchebags and bachelorettes are in fewer supply. The time definitely not to go is on a weekend evening when both food and service are stressed to the max. Whenever you do, get a G&T and that paella and by all means, fill up on tomato bread.

GET THIS

Paella; molecular olives; gin and tonics; sangria; gazpacho; pan de cristal con tomate fresco (tomato bread); José's tuna sandwich; boiled octopus with peewee potatoes; shrimp and lobster fritters; patatas bravas; gambas al ajillo (shrimp with garlic); hanger steak; Iberico ham/sausage selection; endive and goat-cheese salad; salmon with Manchego pisto.

JAPANEIRO (WEST) Asian Fusion

see map 2, page 244
7315 W. Warm Springs Road
(702) 260-8668
facebook.com/Japaneiro
6 p.m.-3 a.m., daily
$25-$75

The flat-out winner of the Best Food in the Worst Location award. Allow us to paint a picture for you.

On a desolate corner in the southwest part of town is a strip mall, one of those L-shaped jobs with spaces for maybe 10 tenants. Japañeiro occupies the corner space, while a few other renters hold on, as they weather the various stages of going into or out of business. There's also a sad-looking video poker bar and a lot of depressing dust and emptiness on the other three corners of Warm Springs and Tenaya. If you were picking the worst place in town to create extraordinary combinations of meat and Asian seafood that would make even the fussiest gourmand sit up and take notice, you couldn't pick one that's more dire.

But survive Kevin Chong has and against all odds. He's done it by bringing in everything from true Belon oysters and live Japanese abalone to Kegani Hokkaido hairy crabs in season. He's done it with technically precise combinations and point-perfect cooking. He's done it by doing Asian fusion food as well or better than anyone on or off the Strip.

Chong previously worked at Nobu and his facility in blending Japanese ideas with in-your-face seasonings shows his pedigree, along with the influence of his sensei, Nobu Matsuhisa. You won't find better kumamoto oysters with uni and foie gras anywhere and that includes Nobu. He toggles back and forth between Asia, France, and the U.S. of A. with equal aplomb, plating gorgeous escargot with

the same flair he shows with giant Nigerian prawns doused with truffle butter and the best beef gyoza in town.

Speaking of meat, you won't find a better cut of beef in the 'burbs than Chong's 24-ounce dry-aged ribeye, sliced and cubed off the bone and served with an array of salts and dried garlic. He also does top-shelf sashimi, a green-tea tiramisu, and fried bananas to beat the band.

Put it all together and you have a unique chef-driven restaurant, the type of place for which foodies are always pining and of which Las Vegas has precious few.

This is not the place to come for bargain-basement fusion food. It is the place for some of the most unique creations in Las Vegas, made by a chef who's passionate about what he does. Chong, like Dan Krohmer at Other Mama, is sourcing Strip-quality ingredients and giving them an East-meets-West spin that always maintains a delicate balance between creativity and understatement. Cooking this fine is worth the tariff, even if a tab for two can get to $150 very quickly; $75 is the price of his multi-course omakase dinner. Ordering a la carte will keep things right around a Benjamin for a couple. Those who blanch at Ben will be happy to know about the happy hour where everything's under five bucks and that the huge ribeye at $65 is a veritable steal.

Location or not, anyone interested in interesting food ought to be eating here.

GET THIS

Sama maru (Japanese mackerel); gyoza; roasted bone marrow; Teramoto scallop; dry-aged ribeye steak; oysters; Nigerian prawns; French escargot; Kumamoto oyster with uni foie gras; salmon ceviche; black cod lettuce wraps; baby squid in miso sauce; hairy crab (in season).

JEAN GEORGES STEAKHOUSE (STRIP) Steakhouse

Aria at CityCenter
(877) 230-2742 / (702) 590-8660
aria.com
5 p.m.-10:30 p.m., daily
$125 and up

They had me at Wagyu brisket.

Actually, Jean-Georges Vongerichten has had me in his thrall since August 30, 1988, when I first tasted his then-groundbreaking Alsace-meets-Asia take on French cuisine in New York City. Back then, he was a wunderkind of Gallic chefs, mixing and matching French technique with the mysterious scents and accents of Thailand. Today, he has dozens of restaurants all over the world, including two of Vegas' best steakhouses. The older one, Prime at Bellagio, will always hold a special place in my heart. For 19 years, it has been Las Vegas' prettiest steakhouse and the food continues to sparkle as much as the room.

Its seven-year-old sibling, the Jean Georges Steakhouse, has always had a more casual vibe. The classic feel of Prime extends to its menu, which changes about as often as I go to a monster truck rally, while at JGS, Vongerichten lets his chefs play with their food. The lucky chef in this case is Sean Griffin, a baby-faced veteran who knows his way around steaks like his boss knows a khao niao from a kai yang.

Griffin's operation hits all the stations on the steakhouse cross (dry-aged, Japanese-raised, grass-grazed), along with the requisite 42-ounce Flintstonean tomahawk chop and the ungodly priced A5 Kobe for those who like to feel their arteries hardening while they eat. As for the brisket, I'll get to that.

But what really distinguishes this place are the little touches Griffin brings to things like a summer fruit salad, egg-on-egg oscetra caviar toast, pepper-crusted foie gras, and a crunchy breast of chicken in a shallow pool of uncommonly good hot sauce. By-the-numbers cooking this is not, whether you're diving into a big lumpy crab cake or a citrusy-glazed sea bass. The steaks are grilled over apricot wood (and finished with rendered beef fat) and take a back seat to no one's, but it's those apps and sides that will get your attention. Summer corn is brought to life by Manchego cheese, chili, and lime, and if there's a better potato dish in town than Griffin's smashed Yukons with jalapeños, I haven't found it.

The aggressive-yet-balanced use of strong tangy accents (peppers, citrus, soy, etc.) distinguish this menu from so many others, including its big brother. These flavors announce JGS as a steakhouse with real kick, one that will keep your palate awake throughout the meal.

Back to that brisket, it's black as coal and smoky as a Texas wildfire. It tiptoes between fork tender and slightly chewy and is all the beef-eatin' a rootin' tootin' carnivore could ask for. It needs a little sauce, but the four they make in house—chili glaze, JG steak sauce, soy miso, and Bearnaise—are all equal to the task.

The desserts are superb and par for the course for a chef who's had my gastronomic attention for half my life.

GET THIS

Caviar on toast; oysters; Dungeness crab cake; foie gras with strawberry-rhubarb jam; Chilean sea bass; crunchy organic chicken; smoked Wagyu brisket; Wagyu tomahawk steak; prime porterhouse; sautéed corn; smashed Yukon potatoes; apple pie; Jean Georges candy bar.

JOEL ROBUCHON (STRIP) French

MGM Grand
(702) 891-7925
mgmgrand.com
5:30-10 p.m., daily
$125 and up

Do you consider yourself a black-belt foodie? Does the thought of a 15-course $500 tasting menu make you moan with pleasure? Are you a belt-notching jetsetter who travels the globe searching for meals to brag about? Does your Instagram page toss off references to Thomas (as in Keller), Ferran (as in Adrià), or Massimo (as in Bottura) as if they were personal friends?

If your answer to any of these questions is "yes," then take comfort in knowing that once you score a table at this pocket of luxury deep in the MGM, you'll be in the company of a few fellow travelers, along, of course, with high-rollers using up a big casino comp with the same blank-eyed efficiency they employ to buy an overpriced purse for the wife, mistress, secretary, or all three. Which is to say you'll eat very well here, but you might find yourself sharing the 50-seat restaurant with people who aren't as ardent about the experience as you are.

Don't blame the restaurant. The chefs and staff go to considerable effort to provide an experience worthy of Joël Robuchon's reputation, and reputations in the food world don't get any higher. But

there's no escaping the fact that you're dining in one of the world's greatest restaurants that happens to be located in a big soulless Las Vegas casino. Once you put that thought to rest (and the soothing décor and hushed tones make it easy to do so), you can settle into a spectacular meal, albeit at a spectacular price.

The good news is you no longer have to go for the 15-course $455 extravaganza. You can get out for around $300 per couple if you want to restrict yourselves to a couple of courses. For our money, the $250 three-course option (the extras expand it to six courses) is the best choice.

Christophe De Lellis holds down the stoves and like his compatriot Jimmy Lesnard next door at L'Atelier, he doesn't look old enough to vote. But what the young man can do with a spit-roasted duck coated in honey and coriander indicates an old-chef's soul.

If you're into comparisons, Robuchon (more refined) competes with Guy Savoy (gutsier) for "best bread cart in the world" honors. Savoy has a greater selection of under $100 wine and it puts out a larger array of perfectly ripe fromages. Pastry chef Alan Mardonovic's cart here is so laden with sweet wonderful goodies you might be tempted to skip the savories altogether. 'Tis a pity they won't let you.

A big deal is made of Robuchon's three-star Michelin status. FYI: Michelin did two books rating Las Vegas restaurants (2008-2009) and hasn't been back since. They're not coming back, either. Despite our 42 million annual visitors, the Las Vegas restaurant guide market is too small (something a certain food writer knows all too well) to justify such an investment. After nine years, any prestigious award would normally seem stale, but in this case, Michelin got it right, and they'll continue to have it right as long as JR keeps chefs like De Lellis and Mardonovic at the helm.

GET THIS

Three-course tasting menu; Menu Degustation; Imperial caviar on white asparagus; sea-urchin flan; truffled langoustine ravioli; scallops in green curry; morel mushrooms in crispy gyoza; semi-soft boiled egg on spinach purée with Comte cheese sauce; sweet and sour vegetables in thin-sliced daikon radish; John Dory in tempura of green shiso; spit-roasted duck with acacia honey and coriander; bread; more bread; desserts; cheese; petit fours.

JULIAN SERRANO (STRIP) Spanish

Aria at CityCenter
(877) 230-2742 / (702) 590-8520
arialasvegas.com
Sun.-Thurs., 11:30 a.m.-10:30 p.m.; Fri.-Sat., 11:30 a.m.-11 p.m.
$25-$75

Julian Serrano and José Andrés don't like each other, which is a shame, because I love them both. I've never delved into it too deeply with either of them, but my guess is that Serrano (a classic at-the-stoves type) thinks of Andrés (the prototypical globetrotting celebrity chef) as a marketer rather than a cook, while Andrés considers Serrano hopelessly old-school. They're both a little bit right, but rather than choosing sides in this Spanish civil war, I prefer to revel in the fact that together, they've given Las Vegas two of the finest tapas restaurants in America. Devotees of each have been known to cross banderillas over who makes the best patatas bravas, but for my money, when I want the classic tastes of España, nothing beats a lunch or dinner at this Aria hotspot. When I want paella and tapas with a more modern twist, I head to Jaleo.

Serrano can get molecular to be sure—witness his ahi tuna on raspberry skewers—but the strengths of his menu lie with his huevos estrellados (fried potatoes, chorizo, and eggs), traditional Spanish croquetas (fried-chicken croquettes oozing Béchamel sauce), and piquillo peppers stuffed with goat cheese. Other don't-miss items include the coca Mallorquina (bready little pizzas covered with melted sharp Mahon cheese over spicy sobrasada sausage), the stuffed Medjol dates, and a layered Spanish tortilla that will take you straight back to Barcelona.

Classic may be its strengths, but new menu items demonstrate a restless kitchen, still revamping and improving a small-plates menu that was plenty strong to begin with. Serrano remains a master of all things foie (as in gras) and his spicy pork meatballs (and I mean spicy) and crab-and-avocado terrine show a culinary titan who's not afraid to innovate. They're also serious about their sherry here, and the bar is constantly coming up with creative killer cocktails.

GET THIS

Patatas bravas; coca Mallorquina; ahi tuna raspberry skewers; Spanish tortilla; stuffed piquillo peppers; huevos estrellados; stuffed Medjol dates; white ceviche; fried calamari; gazpacho; apple manchego salad; fisherman's soup; avocado crab terrine; pork meatballs; Spanish charcuterie platter; pintxo de chorizo; Spanish "pata negra" ham.

KABUTO EDOMAE SUSHI (WEST) Japanese

see map 1, page 243
5040 W. Spring Mountain Road, Suite 4
(702) 676-1044
kabutolv.com
Mon.-Sat., 6-10 p.m.
$75-$125

Kabuto is too good for you. Stop reading right now if you're the sort who's ever swooned over a California roll or had a screaming orgasm over cream cheese and mayonnaise on raw fish. But if you enjoy the real deal—pristine hand-carved slices of exquisite swimmers atop barely warm seasoned rice—then we've got something to talk about.

Real sushi, Edomae (Tokyo-style) sushi, is a relatively new phenomenon. It's only been around a couple of hundred years in Japan and for about three in Vegas. "Edo" is the ancient Japanese word for Tokyo, and it refers to sushi served by the piece, in a serene setting, with mildly vinegared rice and the slightest dab of true wasabi (not that bright green horseradish stuff they smear on in Americanized joints). True sushi can and should be eaten with the fingers. You dip only the fish, ever-so-delicately into the soy, making sure not to sully the rice with all that salt, then pop the whole thing in your mouth. If all of this sounds like an edible form of performance art, congratulations, you're starting to get it.

Real sushi bars are all about the subtle interplay among raw food, minimalist preparation, the chef, and the customer. They're not about stuffing your face with some inside-out roll containing more ingredients than an episode of "Game of Thrones." If you want to eat sushi like a pro, take a seat and go either the Nigiri Omakase ($48 and perfect for beginners) or the Yoroi (intermediate $80) route. The first one gets you only sliced fish on rice of the highest pedigree, while the second throws in sashimi and faultless grilled items for some variety.

Serious sushi hounds go whole hog with the Kabuto menu ($120) that expands all categories and will keep you nailed to your seat with fascination. Sake, the only thing to drink with this food, is expensive by the bottle and gently priced by the carafe. Anyone who drinks red wine with this food should commit seppuku on the spot.

GET THIS

Nigiri Omakase; Yoroi Omakase; Kabuto Omakase; sake by the carafe.

KHOURY'S (WEST) Mediterranean

see map 2, page 244
9340 W. Sahara Avenue,
Suite 106
(702) 671-0005
khouryslv.com
Sun.-Thurs., 11 a.m.-10 p.m.;
Fri.-Sat., 11 a.m.-11 p.m.
$25 or less

We have long admired Khoury's, the Mediterranean/Lebanese restaurant formerly located in the far southwest reaches of the valley. The only thing we didn't like about it was how far it was from our house. Now, it's a bit closer (on West Sahara), having relocated in the past year, and the only thing not to love is how it will spoil you for all other Las Vegas versions of this cuisine. Be forewarned: This city is full of not-so-great Greek/Mediterranean restaurants—a surprising number of which are run by Russians—and industrial gyro meat and tepid tabbouleh are pretty much standard-issue in the 'burbs.

But Khoury's is straight from the old county, in all the best ways. All sausages, pickles, sauces, and pita are made from scratch and the food is aggressively spiced just like they do on the Mediterranean. The house mezze sampler is a nice way to start, and a nice way to feed four to six hungry souls. It's so chock full of goodness (and about a dozen vegetable dishes), you may forget about eating your spiced ground-meat kafta kebabs or the wonderful whole roasted chicken.

Much to the chagrin of my relatives, no Greek in town can top what Khoury's does with fantastic falafel, heavenly hummus, smoky babaganoush, delightful dolmades, luscious loubieh (green beans with garlic and tomatoes), and all sorts of mashed and seasoned cheeses, yogurt, and vegetables. Through it all, you'll be sopping things up with the never-ending baskets of puffy pita—so light, nutty, and addictive you'll inhale two or three of these Mesopotamian marvels as they get replenished to your table straight from the oven. Try not to fill up on bread, and don't miss the sujuk (spicy sausage) pizza, or lahm bi ajeen (ground lamb pizza), either.

That all of this is done in-house, at easy-to-digest prices (almost everything on the menu is well under twenty bucks, except for the meats), is remarkable. That food can taste this good and be so good for you is a blessing from the food gods.

GET THIS

Lahm bi ajeen; sujuk pizza; tabbouleh; hummus; loubieh (green beans); labni-matoon; mtabal babaganoush (fresh grilled eggplants); mezza platters; bamieh (sautéed okra); whole roasted chicken; dolmades; kafta kebabs; pita bread. Lots and lots of pita bread.

L'ATELIER DE JOEL ROBUCHON (STRIP) French

MGM Grand
(702) 891-7358
mgmgrand.com
5-10 p.m., daily
$125 and up

The only thing to dislike about L'Atelier is its infuriatingly inconvenient location. Unless you're staying in the MGM, to get to it, you must first endure the worst parking garage on the Strip or pay through the nose for valet service, run the gauntlet of half-drunk and poorly dressed tourists (or is it the other way around?), then traverse the length of one of the world's largest and most confusing casinos. These annoyances pile up quickly when you're hungry and by the time you actually get to the far reaches of this behemoth of a building, you can be excused for being in a very bad mood. The good news is all will be forgiven as soon as you get a whiff of the place.

The menu can be a bit daunting. There are small bites here and prix-fixes there, and seasonal menus and degustation suggestions, and entrées and appetizers that don't fall in either category. There's even a killer vegetarian menu for those who are so inclined. So, instead of being intimidated or confused, do what I do: Close your eyes and point. No matter what shows up, be it flaky cod with eggplant in a dashi broth, the best lobster salad in the universe, a hanger steak from heaven, or a buttery spaghetti topped with soft-boiled egg, sea urchin, and caviar, you can be assured of a drop-dead-delicious forkful.

L'Atelier, like its big brother Joël Robuchon next door, has been open for 12 years now, and new top toque Jimmy Lesnard (who replaced the beloved Steve Benjamin) has kept things humming along. There is no such thing as perfection—in food or in restaurants—but if a place can be said to put out nearly perfect expressions of the chef's craft, night after night, L'Atelier would be it. I've been here dozens of times and never had a bad meal; I've never even had a bad bite. On second thought, I can almost forgive its inaccessibility. If it was easier to get to, I'd be here every week.

GET THIS

La Morue; flaky cod with eggplant in dashi broth; Le Burger; Ris de Veau (sweetbreads); grilled seasonal vegetables; Les Spaghettis (spaghetti with soft egg, urchin, and caviar); L'Onglet (hanger steak with pommes frites); Le Caille (free-range quail stuffed with foie gras); Le Kampachi (soy-glazed kampachi with endive salad); Le Homard (lobster salad with sherry vinaigrette); Le Jambon (Ibérico de Bellota: Spanish ham with toasted tomato bread). Le Saumon with siracha aioli; eggplant velouté; foie gras parfait with port wine; anything and everything for dessert.

LA CAVE (STRIP) Continental

Wynn Las Vegas
(702) 248-3463
wynnlasvegas.com
Mon.-Thurs., 11:30 a.m.-10 p.m.; Fri. & Sat., 11:30 a.m. to 11 p.m.;
Sunday: brunch 10:30 a.m.-2:30 p.m.; dinner 4 p.m.-10 p.m.
$25-$75

My relationship with the Wynn/Encore is like that of a jilted lover who still stalks his ex-, hopelessly looking for a reconciliation. Ever since these twin towers went full douchebag in 2010, abandoning their great-chefs/great-restaurants mojo in favor of cashing in on the dj-dayclub-nightclub scene, I've watched with the fascination of a brokenhearted boyfriend who sees the girl he used to take to Mozart concerts appear at EDM festivals with sleeve tatts, Molly, and a mohawk. It's not a pretty sight, neither in the hotels (especially on weekends) nor in the restaurants.

As an aside, this doesn't keep them from being the most expensive joints in Vegas. Wynn and his F&B honchos knew enough to establish the brand, compromise quality, hire lesser talent, then expect the customers to still pay through the nose-ring. That part, they got right.

Thankfully, La Cave exists as a respite from all that's unholy surrounding it. How? Simple. It's the only eatery on the premises not owned by the hotel. When you need a respite from the bros, hoes, and slack-jawed Asian tourists (who wander around looking like they don't know what hit them), you can duck into this wine bar and, for a relatively reasonable tariff, enjoy some fabulous food and one of the best wine lists on the Strip.

They call La Cave a wine-and-food hideaway and that pretty much sums it up. Chef Billy DeMarco works wonders out of a teeny tiny kitchen that occupies a sliver of space opposite the bar that offers 50-plus by-the-glass selections at fair prices. You can go nuts sipping or dive into a list stocked with interesting bottles from dozens of countries.

Accompanying your libations will be a variety of nibbles that can astonish. DeMarco's Caesar salad, topped with a crispy prosciutto chip, is a marvel of vertical engineering, as is another unlikely high-flier: his bacon-and-egg fettucine. He does wonders with all sorts of standards as well, from salt-roasted beets with whipped goat cheese to a tangy gorgonzola salad, all geared toward adroit pairings with various wines that the sommeliers will happily steer you to. In cooler weather, the mushroom grits with pecorino cheese and onion soup should not be missed, and no matter what the temperature outside, your table will be fighting over the jumbo lump crab in lettuce cups and the snappy Thai snapper ceviche. The flatbreads are all worthy of the top-shelf wines being poured, and the seared mini-burgers or sliced sirloin are just the ticket to pair with whatever big-or-small-ticket pinot noir suits your fancy.

One thing for which we can give credit to the Wynn is giving most of its eateries a beautiful outdoor patio and La Cave has one of the prettiest.

This oasis isn't cheap, but compared to the rest of the hotel, it feels like a bargain. No one here is just going through the motions when it comes to putting out the food and you won't need to schedule an appointment with your proctologist after you get the bill.

GET THIS

Jumbo lump crab lettuce cups; all flatbreads; Thai snapper sashimi, mini-burgers; sliced sirloin steak; bacon and egg fettucine; Caesar salad; gorgonzola salad; salt-roasted beets; mushroom grits; onions soup sunny side organic egg; bacon-wrapped dates; cheese platter; beignets; s'mores; crème brûlée.

LE CIRQUE (STRIP) French

Bellagio
(702) 693-8100
bellagio.com
5:30-10 p.m., daily
$75-$125

If two restaurants can be said to have jump-started our food revolution, Spago and Le Cirque must be given the credit. Spago got the ball rolling in 1992, but Le Cirque's arrival in 1998 caused a seismic shift in our taste tectonics. As good as the rest of Steve Wynn's eateries at Bellagio were (Picasso, Prime, Olives, et al.), he knew he needed a big hitter from the Big Apple to really get the food-world's attention. Enter the Maccioni family, bringing with them what was, at the time, the most famous name in American restaurants.

With the Maccionis patrolling the room and paterfamilias Sirio making constant appearances from New York, Las Vegas was a satellite operation, but every bit the equal of its hallowed namesake. A succession of great chefs has kept this kitchen firing on all cylinders and one of the best service staffs in the business keeps the dining room humming. I was afraid all that might come to an end in 2013 when the management deal with the family ended. With Sirio deep into his eighties now and son Mario gone, the operation is a licensing rather than a management deal—more Bellagio, less Maccioni. The good news is neither the food nor the service has suffered for it.

Credit for that crackerjack service goes to a team that has barely changed in 19 years. If you came here when Bill Clinton was president and returned today, you'd see all the same faces serving you. Frederic Montandon still pours vintages (French, please! California, if you insist) with a twinkle in his eye, while Ivo Angelov manages with the touch of an orchestra conductor. A lot of restaurants feel stale after two decades. Not here.

The food has changed over time, but never wavered. Some of the chefs (Poidevin, David Werly, and Wil Bergerhausen) were superstars in their own right, while others were just putting in their time. But whoever was at the helm, the kitchen has always been solid, rendering classics like rack of lamb with glazed sweetbreads and rabbit with mustard cream sauce with the same aplomb it devotes to gold-crusted quail stuffed with foie gras or blue crab under a robe of caviar. You can still get a lobster salad here that is almost note-for-note what Daniel Boulud invented in 1988 or have your taste buds startled by ex-chef Bergerhausen's "hidden" spring garden of English peas, tendrils, and garbanzos misted with strawberries.

What used to be dueling menus of Le Cirque classics versus more modern (read: lighter) fare has expanded into four offerings at all price ranges. You can do everything from a $108 pre-theater affair to a $350 extravaganza that steps into the ring with whatever punches Savoy, Gagnaire, or Robuchon are throwing and doesn't flinch. A delicious-sounding five-course vegetarian menu ($115) looks like a good idea, in the same way that yoga classes, wheat grass, and prostate exams do.

Every night seems like New Year's Eve here. High rollers, celebrities, and hedonic jetsetters treat this place like a private club, making a reservation tough on weekends. Personally, I like to go in early mid-week, grab a seat at the bar, and watch the choreography. After almost two decades, the balletic grace of Le Cirque is still something to behold.

GET THIS

Oysters; lobster salad "Le Cirque"; Maryland blue crab with caviar; Savoyard sunchoke soup; foie gras with tapioca; seasonal risotto; braised veal cheeks; roasted chicken; sea bass in potato crust; A5 Wagyu strip with bordelaise sauce; gold-crusted quail farci; rabbit with mustard sauce; sweetbreads; "hidden" spring garden salad; vegetarian tasting menu.

LIBERTINE SOCIAL (STRIP) American

Mandalay Bay
(702) 632-7558 / (702) 632-7800
mandalaybay.com
5-10:30 p.m., daily
$25-$75

A sprawling restaurant-bar somehow manages to capture the small-plates and craft-cocktail zeitgeist of the past half-decade without feeling soulless or derivative. It's a big-casino concept restaurant to be sure, but it's one that feels like a hangout—with personality to spare and intimacy beyond what you'd expect in a huge "concept" eatery.

The concept at hand was dreamed up by Shawn McClain (of Sage and Chicago fame) and über-mixmeister Tony Abou-Ganim. McClain designed the food, TAG the booze, and between them, they've hit a number of nails of the head.

Small plates being so 2010, this joint could've ended up featuring one cliché after the other, but here, McClain and Executive Chef Richard Camarota manage to make them sing without lapsing into the same-old shared-meal doldrums. There's plenty to pass around here, but boredom isn't on the menu.

Olives get wrapped in sausage, churros get a savory parmesan spin, and gazpacho is served as strawberry shots with crab meat: It's a typical, all-over-the-map, Millennial-friendly menu, but it never feels like it was borrowed from a Kerry Simon restaurant. Nor does it skimp on modernist complexity, such as in these "modern fried eggs," a choice of eternally eggy pleasures, none of them fried, but all of them fascinating. Equally compelling are the flatbreads, one made with real guanciale and garlic oil, another displaying strips of real country ham set off by smoked blue cheese, pineapple, and barbecue sauce. It may sound like an overwrought mess, but it all works: That salty ham also helps whet the appetite for plenty of well-crafted cocktails (more on this in a minute).

The double-cheeseburger is a dream, oozing with melted "Kraft-ed" cheese sauce, and the faked-named "American Kobe" flat-iron makes up in beefy succulence for what it lacks in honest advertising.

All sins are atoned for, however, when the booze starts flowing. Abou-Ganim is one of maybe a half-dozen Americans who can truly be called cocktail icons. Like his buddy Dale DeGroff, he was in on the ground floor of our mixology Renaissance and putting him in charge of the bar here was a wise move indeed.

Whether you want a lesson in properly mixed booze or just to get sloshed, you'll be in for a treat. Drinks come in a dizzying array of variety and packaging: old-school (hello Harvey Wallbanger!), flavored, barrel-aged, and even bottled. Fifteen well-chosen beers are on tap, with cocktails on draft as well. For our money, though, the things to get are the fizzes and the swizzlers. Like the name implies, the fizzes showcase four or five ingredients given just the right of spritz to make them slide down your gullet like a stripper on a pole.

GET THIS

Modern house-baked pretzel; fried egg; avocado panzanella; warm crab dip; wood-grilled sausages; roasted beets; beef tartare; Libertine cheeseburger; country ham flatbread; olives in sausage; gazpacho with crab; skirt steak; barbecued carrots; coal-charred corn; Manhattan bread pudding; Margarita donuts; swizzle cocktails for four.

LOTUS OF SIAM (EAST) Thai

see map 1, page 243
953 E. Sahara Avenue,
Suite A5
(702) 538-6135
lotusofsiamlv.com
Mon.-Fri., 11 a.m.-2:30 p.m.;
5:30-10 p.m., daily
$25-$75

Yogi Berra once said: "That place is so crowded, no one goes there anymore." Truer words were never spoken about LOS.

Ever since Bill and Saipin Chutima took over this space in 1999, it seems every gourmet in the world has beaten a path to their door. So popular has it become with the fiery-foods crowd that a table is almost impossible to score on a weekend evening—when you'll see taxi after taxi dropping off parties large and small every few minutes as tourists make their pilgrimage here to sample our most famous off-the-Strip eatery.

In no other Thai restaurant in town can you find the variety, freshness, and vivid flavors put forth by this kitchen on a daily basis. (Those who had judged Lotus by its lunch buffet were missing the point of this restaurant. Thankfully, they finally discontinued their tepid ode to the all-you-can-eat-crowd a couple of years ago. These days, if you show up for lunch, which also can be crowded if you don't arrive before noon, you get the same menu as the one served at dinner.) The point of Lotus is and always has been the northern and Issan specialties (all in English on the menu), done the way Saipin's mother taught her and well enough to garner her two James Beard Award nominations and (finally), in 2011, the award for Best Chef Southwest (shared with Claude Le Tohic of Joël Robuchon). Pair these dishes with the extraordinary Rieslings that make up one of the best German wine lists in the country.

Add it all up and you have an experience that earns the distinction of being called the best Thai food in the U.S. by Jonathon Gold of the *Los Angeles Times*. Unlike Mr. Gold, I haven't been to every Thai restaurant in the country, but I do tend to agree with him on that score, especially when lingering over bites of Issan sour sausage, koi soi (raw beef with chiles), or Chutima's definitive northern Thai curries. Warning: Gringos should avoid asking for anything "Bangkok hot."

GET THIS

Issan sour sausage; kang hung lay (just because we like saying it); miam kham; khao soi (curry noodles); drunken noodle prawns; catfish larb; nam kao tod (crunchy rice with raw cured pork and peanuts); Panang braised beef; all curries; northern Thai sausage; mango with sticky rice; anything off the northern Thai or Issan menus; any white German or Austrian wine on the phenomenal list, the prices of which are a flat-out steal.

MARCHE BACCHUS (WEST) French

see map 2, page 244
2620 Regatta Drive, Suite 106
(702) 804-8008
marchebacchus.com
Lunch: Mon.-Sat., 11 a.m.-3:30 p.m.; Brunch: Sun., 10 a.m.-3:30 p.m.
Sun.-Tues., 4-8:30 p.m.; Wed.-Thurs., 4-9 p.m.; Fri.-Sat., 4-9:30 p.m.
$25-$75

A proper lunch in the suburbs is harder to find than a corkscrew at BYU. Las Vegans don't do lunch, not the way New York or Portland does lunch. Las Vegas' professional classes (to the extent they exist) are too busy filling up on Subway sandwiches to think about lunch. (An exotic power lunch at an old law firm of mine consisted of four partners eating cheeseburgers and pontificating to us underlings over iced teas at Red Robin. Good times.) Lunch in Las Vegas is such a sad and desperate affair that people have been known to travel 15 miles from the Strip to an obscure shopping center on a fake lake to find a small red sign tucked in a corner over a modest doorway that says, Marché Bacchus. They do this because this is one of the few places where civilized people dine—as opposed to just pumping fuel into their tanks—at midday.

Before you get to the food, though, you'll have to navigate the wine store. A wall of pinot noir stands to your right and the floor before you is lined with three rows of wooden bins bulging with bottles. A large wine store it's not, but the selections are carefully chosen, with labels galore at every price range, by the owners, Rhonda and Jeff Wyatt. Oenophiles will have a field day while lesser imbibers and teetotalers are being led to their seats. No matter where you fall on the alcohol-consumption continuum, you'll be charmed by the setting and décor—so charmed, in fact, that you might adopt this as your favorite off-Strip restaurant before you've even taken your first bite.

Whether you come for lunch, brunch, or dinner, you and your guests will find plenty of solid cooking to choose from. Most of the large menu skews toward classic French-bistro fare (steak frites, escargot "persillade," and the like), but plenty of pastas and salads satisfy the pickiest crowd. Francophiles won't want to miss the croque monsieur, quiche Lorraine, or onion soup; carnivores go ga-ga over the burger and steak tartare; and those who insist on Italian won't find any fault with the bucatini amatriciana or vegetable ravioli. The brunch menu is more egg-centric, but as good as the Benedicts and goat-cheese omelets are, we prefer meatier fare like the truffled grits and beef grillade, the better to go with all those fabulous red wines at your fingertips for only $10 over the retail price. Because of this very gentle pricing policy, MB has made itself the go-to joint for sommeliers and serious sippers, from all over town and all over the country.

The reason I'm going on about lunch is because lunch is the best time to come to MB. The service is more relaxed, the food is just as good, and lingering by the pond and watching the ducks paddle about is the perfect way to while away an afternoon while your co-workers are swooning over Pizza Hut at their desks. There's no better place in southern Nevada to have an affair, entertain Grandma, drink wine, or play hooky.

GET THIS

Charcuterie platter; cheese platter; French onion soup; quiche Lorraine; escargot "persillade"; croque madame; truffled grits & beef grillades; Prince Edward Island mussels; goat cheese napoleon; steak tartare with quail egg; steak frites; bucatini amatriciana; vegetable ravioli; honey-spiced glazed duck breast; bistro chicken; buckwheat crêpes; Bacchus omelette; smoked salmon Benedict; Bacchus bread pudding.

MICHAEL MINA (STRIP) Seafood

Bellagio
(702) 693-8865
bellagio.com
Mon.-Sat., 5:30-10 p.m.
$75-$125

I like to call Michael Mina the Egyptian Wolfgang Puck, and he fits the bill for several reasons. First and foremost is his ability to pull off multiple concepts at all price points, while never losing his street cred as one of the most talented chefs in the business. Secondly, while he's serving up everything from sushi (at Pabu in San Francisco) and football fans at 49ers' games to textbook-perfect French classics (e.g., Bardot Brasserie), he never loses sight of the seafood that made him famous. And finally, like Puck, Mina always makes sure his number-one brand is always in top form. With Puck, that would be Spago and with Mina, it's his eponymous restaurants in San Fran and Bellagio. After long runs in both cities, neither seems to miss a beat, and if you stroll into our MM, you'll find it remains as chic and timeless as a Chanel dress.

The Tony Chi design has aged remarkably well and to these eyes is as elegant as ever, remaining one of the most flattering and comfortable rooms in the business. Just as good is Mina's cuisine: a bit less seafood-centric than a decade ago, but just as carefully wrought and beautifully presented.

Start with the tableside-mixed tuna tartare (everyone does), then throw caution (and your cardiologist's advice) to the wind and order the whole lobe of foie gras. Yep, a whole foie, both lobes, roasted to a "T" and carved tableside to the oohs and aahs and envy of everyone else in the dining room. It's as decadent a way to enjoy dinner as there is, but hey, you're in Vegas!

Once you're done hardening your arteries and pissing off the PETA crowd, kick back with a lobster pot pie, still a show stopper after 17 years. Mina never met a piece of pisces he didn't know how to improve upon, and the balance he brings to his sauces and side dishes is extraordinary. P.S. The steaks and lamb are pretty damn good, too.

GET THIS

Tuna tartare; whole foie gras; lobster pot pie, wild king salmon; seasonal tasting menu.

MOREL'S STEAKHOUSE & BISTRO (STRIP) French

Palazzo
(702) 607-6333
palazzo.com
Mon.-Thurs., 8 a.m.-11 p.m.; Fri.-Sat., 8 a.m.-midnight; Sun., 8 a.m.-10 p.m.
$75-$125

The best three-meal-a-day restaurant in town that no one ever talks about. No matter when you show up, be it for brunch or a cholesterol-fest, expect to be quietly blown away by your meal. Restaurants that stretch their kitchens from eggs Benedict to rigatoni Bolognese usually do so out of desperation and rarely do all of it well. Here, you'll be just as impressed by your fish and chips (best in Vegas) as the pancakes and turkey hash. They do all the requisite corn-fed, grass-fed, dry-aged beef here (as well as superb chicken and rack of lamb), but there's also a fondue on the menu that's cheese-eating at its best. Speaking of les fromage, they have a nice selection here, and are one of the few restaurants that feature the fermented curd as part of your dining experience. The raw bar doesn't threaten Bouchon for oyster preeminence, but puts out a more than respectable seafood selection. You can't go wrong with the marinated octopus salad (or any of the salads) either. Put it all together and you have a big white-tablecloth restaurant that is so jaw-droppingly pleasing, on so many levels, that it's become our go-to default eatery whenever we're trying to please a big crowd.

Right across the casino floor is its competition, one of those franchised something-for-everyone restaurants (I think it's called the Grand Cheesecake Café or something) that I hold in the highest contempt—serving up a gazillion covers a day of Sysco slop to slack-jawed hordes who demand little but predictability. If they allowed themselves (and were willing to spend a few more bucks), they could taste the real thing instead of food made by an accountant with a computer. Only a two-minute stroll away is a real tableside-made Caesar, gorgeously trimmed steaks, luscious crabmeat cocktail, mac & (real) cheese, and food made 18 hours a day by real chefs who take pride in their work. Instead, the hoi polloi pack themselves in a food factory so they can eat the same boring crap they get in Bumfudge, Utah. Every time he sees the lines out the door waiting for that franchised dreck, the baby Jesus cries a little.

GET THIS

Fish and chips; Dungeness crab cocktail; fondue; tableside Caesar salad; snap-pea Caesar; octopus salad; rigatoni Bolognese; strip steak, rack of lamb; eggs Benedict; turkey hash; burger; French onion soup "poutine"; mac & cheese; oysters; cheese platter; chocolate tarte; profiteroles; tableside Bloody Mary; made-to-order chocolate mousse.

MR CHOW (STRIP) Chinese

Caesars Palace
(702) 731-7888
caesarspalace.com
Sun.-Thurs., 5-10 p.m.; Fri.-Sat., 5-10:30 p.m.
$75-$125

Mr. Chow (the man) has been servicing the jet-set glitterati for 40 years, serving them upscale versions of "Beijing cuisine," eaten with forks and knives, in turgid white-tablecloth surroundings that insulate them from the messy realities of real Chinese food and the unwashed masses who might enjoy it. At this, the man is a genius.

MR CHOW (the restaurant) is a place food critics have always loved to hate. That is, until now. Because this fussy connoisseur considers it (along with Carbone, its spiritual Italian cousin) to be a perfect match with Sin City. So perfect, in fact, that we wonder why it took so long for them to get here. This being Vegas, of course, the exclusivity and velvet rope-thing must take a back seat to filling the seats. But fill them they do, in one of our most dramatic dining rooms—a setting that fits this town like a man-bun on a Mongolian.

The circular dining room gives everyone a view of the show—who's coming and going and ordering the $225 Peking duck. The whiteness of the space provides flattering lighting for you and the food, and the size and thickness of the linens tell you you're in for an upscale Asian experience like you (and Las Vegas) have never seen before. The food (that critics from London to Los Angeles have trashed) is about as authentic as a fortune cookie, but none the worse for it. What Michael Chow aims for is elegant versions of both peasant and Mandarin dishes from the Chinese repertoire. Thus will you find superb dim sum, serious squab in lettuce cups, and minced-beef pancakes that are as far from your neighborhood sweet-and-sour palace as Caesars is from Motel 6. Certain hors d'oeuvres , like the chicken curry and turnip puffs, aren't worth the $15 tariff, but most of the menu makes sense if you come with a crowd and share.

What everyone will want to share is the dressed Dungeness crab, a snow-white pillow of egg whites holding big chunks of sweet crab, and the oddly named With Three, a stir fry of calves liver, big prawns, and chicken that somehow works. Couples (and those not wanting to spring for the whole bird) will enjoy the smaller portion of Gamblers Duck that's just as crispy, if not as finely tuned, as the show stopper. Both the fluorescent green prawns and the steamed Dover sole will make you sit up and take notice as well.

Purists may balk, but MR CHOW is about unabashed big-deal meal service, a luminous setting, and a sense you're being fed by, and dining with, grownups. It's a throwback in all the right ways, and just the ticket if you value feeling pampered at a price.

GET THIS

Green prawns; squab with lettuce; minced beef pancake; shrimp dumplings; lobster shumai; MR CHOW noodles; With Three; Dover sole; Gamblers Duck; Peking duck; dressed Dungeness crab; crispy beef.

OTHER MAMA (WEST) Raw Bar

see map 2, page 244
3655 South Durango, Suite 6
(702) 463-8382
othermamalv.com
5-11 p.m., daily
$25-$75

Location counts, except when it doesn't. Other Mama may be harder to find than a celebrity chef in the kitchen, but that hasn't stopped every galloping gastronome around from zeroing in on this hidden gem, tucked into an invisible corner in a generic strip mall on South Durango. In a matter of weeks after it opened, Dan Krohmer's ode to great seafood went from "Where's/what's that?" to "Let's go" on the lips of every foodie in town. These days, it's practically a hangout for off-duty chefs and F&B professionals, as well as the go-to joint for locals seeking serious shellfish.

Nothing about its obscure locale suggests that you're in for top-flight oysters, Penn Cove mussels, or sashimi-grade scallops when you find it. Nor does the name give you a clue—it sounds like a blues bar, and the retro-louche signage suggests a down-on-its-heels absinthe joint you might find in New Orleans. Even when you walk in, things are bit confusing. It's modestly appointed (Krohmer did the build-out himself) with seating for around 50, and the far wall is dominated by a long L-shaped cocktail bar that looks directly into an open kitchen. That bar may look simple, but it's also significant,

with mixologist David English shaking, stirring, and conjuring cocktails to a fare-thee-well.

Then you notice a large menu board and things start falling in place. Other Mama is an American/Japanese izakaya/sushi/raw bar/gastropub. Got that? Krohmer cut his seafood teeth with Iron Chef Morimoto (in Philadelphia) and honed his skills locally at Sen of Japan, just down the street. He specializes in strong flavors paired with impeccably chosen seafood, such as his oysters foie Rockefeller—a dish that combines sweet and salty bivalves with an umami-bomb of duck liver. Everything from the raw bar—from amberjack crudo with Meyer lemon and scallop carpaccio to a sashimi salad with thyme and honey—competes with anything you'll find 10 miles to the east at two-thirds the price, and his pork-belly kimchee fried rice, seafood toban yaki, and caviar French toast prove Krohmer can pull together proteins and starches in unlikely combinations as well.

Gone are the days when all-you-can-eat sushi bars defined our fish eating off the Strip. Almost overnight, Other Mama upped everyone's game and put to rest the idea that you have to travel to Las Vegas Boulevard South to get the good stuff.

GET THIS

Oysters foie Rockefeller; amberjack crudo; pork-belly kimchee fried rice; Penn Cove mussels.

PICASSO [STRIP] French/Spanish

Bellagio
(702) 693-7223
bellagio.com
Wed.-Mon., 5:30-9:30 p.m.
$125 and up

When you're at Picasso, all feels right with the world. Sitting on the outdoor patio watching the dancing waters (one of the most romantic venues anywhere) or tucked into one of the comfy chairs beneath millions of dollars' worth of Pablo's handiwork, it's hard to have a care or concern other than how good your meal is going to be. As the story goes, when Steve Wynn lost the Bellagio in a hostile takeover, one of the conditions placed upon the sale was that the Picassos remain in this restaurant. Whether this is a good or bad thing is relative: Without the museum-quality paintings, there would be nothing to stare at but the food and the water. On the other hand, Julian Serrano's cuisine is so artful it more than handles the competition.

Two huge Picassos dominate the bar area, but reserve your art-appreciation lessons for after the meal. That's when most people stroll around the restaurant, casually checking out stuff that usually hangs in the Prado or MOMA. They may be "minor Picassos," as one insufferable snob once told me, but they're the real deal and it's doubtful better art hangs in any restaurant anywhere in the world.

For the price of a prix fixe (four-course) or degustation (five-course) menu (or even just a cocktail at the intimate bar), all this culture is yours for the taking.

Before you get to the food, though, you'll be confronted by a wine list the size of a coffee-table picture book. The surroundings may scream "Sticker Shock Ahead!" but take some time with this tome and you'll find plenty to drink at prices that won't have you reaching for a respirator.

Between the wine, cocktails, and art, there are distractions aplenty here. The good news is they all serve to enhance what's on your plate. For 19 years now, Julian Serrano and his number one, Yoshi Honda, have put out two streamlined menus that astonish as much as they satisfy. No matter what you order, expect the dishes to walk a tightrope between precision and gutsiness. Serrano knows his audience (naïve tourists, intrepid foodies, expense-account fat cats) and he aims to satisfy all comers with great ingredients handled to display primary flavors, not plating pirouettes.

Since day one, he has featured the best U-10 day-boat scallops on Earth, gorgeous poached oysters, and a veal chop to end all arguments. The accents and sides change with the seasons, so expect to find roasted lobster in the summer and meaty breast of pigeon with wild-rice risotto in the fall. Foie gras gets torqued into a cool torchon or sautéed like a precious steak. Both are surpassingly good and would cause a riot if they were taken off the menu. Whether it's warm quail salad, a meaty cylinder of king crab with horseradish, or Colorado lamb with mint aioli, the food, including the seasonal desserts of Matthew Fleisher, is always as finely rendered as the brushstrokes surrounding it. There is an almost Japanese-like exactitude to this cooking and its attention to detail. It may not be the most inventive meal you have in Las Vegas, but it will be the most flawless.

GET THIS

Maine lobster salad; poached oysters; U-10 day-boat scallop; foie gras; Colorado lamb tournedos; veal chop; warm quail salad; roasted pigeon; medallions of fallow deer; sautéed black bass; dessert; wine.

PRIME (STRIP) Steakhouse

Bellagio
(702) 693-7223
bellagio.com
5-10 p.m., daily
$75-$125

Prime has been around for 17 years and would be considered just another superior Vegas steakhouse if all the other food it serves wasn't so jaw-droppingly great and the décor the most stunning in the steakhouse business. That décor blends blue and brown in all sorts of romance-enhancing, conversation-inducing, meat-friendly ways. It's not only the prettiest steakhouse in which you'll ever enjoy a ribeye, but also the most comfortable. Everything about the place is designed to soothe and satisfy—from the greeting and the patio (score a table by the water if you can) to food that does the Jean-Georges Vongerichten brand proud.

None of this comes cheap, but you won't find better steaks and sauces anywhere in town, complemented by vegetables and sides that would make a perfect meal all by themselves. Ribbons of tuna swimming in a ginger marinade take your breath away, as do the onion soup and any of the artfully composed salads.

As good as these standards are—can a peppercorn-crusted strip steak with Béarnaise sauce get any better?—the Parmesan-crusted chicken is the real sleeper on the menu. It's a dish most fowl: moist,

crispy, and full of chicken-ness (nope, it doesn't taste like chicken; it tastes like *chicken*), and it's a dish even Italian chefs should envy for its crust, cheese, and crackle. The wine list, however, is not for the faint of heart or the parsimonious of pocket.

GET THIS

Onion soup; ribbons of tuna; Dungeness crab cake; seared foie gras with sweet-and-sour morels; Caesar salad; baby iceberg lettuce with Maytag blue cheese; Parmesan-crusted chicken; peppercorn-crusted New York strip; dry-aged bone-in ribeye; pan-roasted Dover sole; duck à l'Orange; every single sauce and every single potato dish.

RAKU & SWEETS RAKU (WEST) Japanese

see map 1, page 243
5030 Spring Mtn. Road Suites 2 & 3
(702) 367-3511 / (702) 290-7181
raku-grill.com
Raku: Mon.-Sat., 6 p.m.-2 a.m. / Sweets Raku: Thurs.-Tues., 6 p.m.-midnight; Sat., noon-midnight; Sun., noon-9 p.m.
$25-$75

Raku and Sweets Raku aren't simply places to eat; they're statements of quality and passion, a dedication to excellence that can no longer be faked or phoned in, either on or off the Strip. You can thank Japanese émigré Mitsuo Endo for this taste revolution (not some absentee celebrity chef who treats Vegas like an easy-access ATM machine). The next great meal you have off the Strip, be it a humble noodle joint or a fancy chef-driven room, owes more than a little nod to Endo-san's continuing quest for perfection. It was he who made Spring Mountain Road a foodie destination, lifting it above its roots as a forlorn stretch of bargain-basement Asian eats.

Japanese izakaya, oden, and robata cooking was virtually unheard of when Raku opened in early 2008. With only his authentic sensibilities to guide him, Endo has taught Las Vegas just how great Japanese cooking can be. Izakayas are everywhere these days, strutting their stuff and educating palates like nobody's business, but Raku, hidden in a corner of a small Spring Mountain Road strip mall, gave Las Vegas its first taste of binchotan charcoal cooking and pork

cheek, beef silver skin, and tomato with bacon and asparagus, which are just as stunning today as they were when the place opened. The agedashi tofu and foie gras egg custard are studies in steamed minimalism, and what this tiny kitchen does with oily fish is legendary. There's a fixed menu of all of the above, but true Japronauts wait for the daily-specials chalk board to come around, then just point and enjoy the ride.

Raku is for a certain type of adventuresome food lover, but its sweet sister parked a few doors down serves finely crafted desserts (and small savory bites, and lunch on weekends) that can either be analyzed, admired for their art, or consumed wholesale, depending on your mood. French technique blended with Japanese precision is a match made in heaven and Sweets Raku takes a back seat to no one when it comes to eye-popping sugar creations.

Endo-san may not be aware of the revolution he started, but I am. *Domo arigato* and *gochisousama* ("Thank you for feeding us"), Mitsuo Endo.

GET THIS

Raku: Agedashi tofu; Kobe beef liver sashimi; ayu nanbantsuke (sweet marinated smelt); beef silver skin ebishinjo (shrimp) souffle; kurobuta pork cheek; fried ice fish; sashimi salad; Raku tofu; poached egg with sea urchin and salmon roe; sunomono salad; Tsukune-grilled ground chicken; Kobe beef liver.

Sweets Raku: Seasonal dessert set; les fromages japonaise; foie gras.

RESTAURANT GUY SAVOY (STRIP) French

Caesars Palace
(702) 731-7286
caesarspalace.com
Wed.-Sun., 5:30-9:30 p.m.
$125 and up

A meal at Restaurant Guy Savoy is an event. You can feel it as you approach the giant dark doors down the tucked-away hallway and you can sense it as you're led into the cathedral-like space boasting what may be the tallest ceiling in gastronomia. But once you're seated, you'll share the room with only a few other souls.

Economist Tyler Cowen has counseled avoiding any restaurant where "groups of people (especially beautiful women) are laughing loudly and having a good time," indicating people are there for anything but the food. You'll never encounter this at RGS. Here, the tones will be hushed and the reverence palpable. Like its competitor Joël Robuchon down the street, there is a sense of food being cooked, plated, and consumed as part of a secular religion. Robuchon is like a temple of fine dining, while Savoy is more of a chapel (that high-ceiling thing again.) Regardless, the patrons here are very serious about what they eat and drink.

Top toque Julien Asseo now oversees all the classics that made Guy famous—"Peas All Around," "Colors of Caviar," artichoke truffle soup, and Guinea hen au cocotte—but also exotica like "Santa

Barbara spot prawns caught in a sweet-and-sour fishnet" (a blanket of mesh-cut daikons) or wild salmon "cooked" on a slab of dry ice, a conceit brought tableside that turns the fish into a dense tooth-someness unknown to most fish lovers.

French chefs know foie gras like Koreans know cabbage and Asseo and his brigade de cuisine are no slouches in this arena, offering small cubes of horseradish-topped foie over poached celery stalks dressed with "potato-chip bouillon," a dish that tastes exactly like it sounds. Modernist touches are scattered here and there, for example lobster, beets, and crab bathed with "cold steam," but what keeps us coming back are the classics, such as veal three ways and a mosaic of milk-fed poularde and foie gras, circular discs of the finest grained paté you can imagine. In fall, there is the famous pumpkin soup served from the gourd and showered with white truffles. The turbot a la plancha with sea urchin and black rice is a treat no matter what season it is, and the bread and cheese carts are the stuff of which dreams are made.

Accompanying it all is the biggest and best wine list in town—so big it needs its own table and so good you'll be able to find the perfect bottle in the $75-$125 range as easily as a cult Cabernet or a classified growth. Anyone who drinks anything but wine with this food needs to have their head examined.

Restaurants like Guy Savoy, Joël Robuchon, and Twist don't really have any competition in town. These Big Three compete only with one another and themselves. As the only American outposts of three of the most iconic French chefs on Earth, there is preciseness on the plate that few places in the world can match. Savoy's menu may not be as innovative as Gagnaire's or as involved as Robuchon's, but on any night of the week, its ingredients and cooking stand shoulder to shoulder with them.

Las Vegas is lucky to have all three within a mile of one another. I'm lucky that each is only ten minutes from my house.

GET THIS

Marinated grilled hamachi with egg-sherry vinegar; eggplant sherry and radish gelée; mosaic of milk-fed poularde; oysters en gelée; pintade (guinea fowl); Peas All Around, truffle-artichoke soup; Colors of Caviar; turbot a la plancha; lobster and lump crab in cold steam; salmon "iceberg"; veal three ways; bread and cheese, then more bread and more cheese; wine.

ROSALLIE LE FRENCH CAFE (WEST) French

see map 2, page 244
6090 S. Rainbow Boulevard
(702) 998-4121
rosallie.com
7 a.m.-6 p.m., daily
$25 or less

Driving around Las Vegas can be depressing. Mile after mile of soulless strip malls, gas stations, and the relentless infestation of franchises can sap the spirit of even the heartiest food explorer. Some cities pride themselves on their history and culinary traditions; Las Vegas prides itself on having a Walgreen's on every corner.

Amidst all the crass commercialism, however, are little gems of individualism, oases of good eating where dedicated artisans buck the odds (and greedy real estate developers) and endeavor to put out handmade products of uncompromising quality. This tiny bakery-café sits like an island of ethereal pastries, quiches, sandwiches, and desserts in a sea of empty lots and ugly office buildings in the southwest part of town. There's absolutely no reason to think that it would be something special (the other "French cafés" around town are mostly gawdawful), but once you bite into Jonathan Pluvinet's caneles de Bordeaux, quiche Lorraine, or tartine Provencale, you'll be transported—not just out of your hot dusty surroundings, but to a sidewalk in southern France where they take this type of eating for granted.

Why are the sandwiches so good? Because they use bread that came out of the oven that morning. If there's a better croissant sandwich than his croque Rosallie, made with Parisian ham and sweet-onion Bechamel, I haven't found it. The quiches are both intensely eggy and light (no mean feat) and the pastries are otherworldly. Pluvinet,

who is French through and through, learned baking at his parent's knee and doesn't know how to make compromises.

Remember that scene in *Ratatouille* where Anton Ego takes a bite of Remy's food and is flooded with taste memories of days gone by? That's the way I felt when I first tried Pluvinet's pain au chocolat. Yeah, it's that good.

GET THIS

Croissant; pain au chocolat; cheese Danish; caneles de Bordeaux; quiches, croque Rosallie; tartine Normandie; apple tarte; apple croustade; palmiers; almond-nutella tarte; raspberry linzer pie; plateau de fromage; country sausage plate; espresso; cappuccino.

SAGE (STRIP) Contemporary

Aria at CityCenter
(877) 230-2742
aria.com
Mon.-Sat., 6-10:30 p.m.
$75-$125

If Sage were in any other foodie capital in America (including such bastions of snobbery like New York and San Francisco), it would be considered one of the best restaurants in town. If it were in Portland, Austin, or Pittsburgh, it would be considered the best restaurant in town. If it weren't located in a huge Las Vegas hotel, it would've won a James Beard Award by now, and if frogs had wings, they wouldn't thump their asses against the ground. Shed no tears for Shawn McClain and his executive chef Chris Heisinger, however, because they're content to run what is, along with Guy Savoy, a cathedral of fine food that demands precise attention to the catechisms occurring on the plate. If you've ever wondered about the best way to roast a carrot, brûlée some foie gras, grill some octopus, or serve lamb belly with romesco, merguez sausage, and pomegranate, they've got the answers.

The first thing you notice about Sage is how tall it is. Its 20-foot façade and ceilings announce some serious intentions. Likewise, the long bar—backed by a wall of serious spirits, including a fabulous selection of bourbons—is so sleek and welcoming that it makes me wish I were an alcoholic. You'll be tempted to park yourself at a stool and let the bartenders dazzle you with their footwork. Also tempting is the bar menu itself: something of a microcosm of the main room, showing off this kitchen's facility with oysters, eggs, scallops, and hanger steak. You could just nibble and sip there and die happy, but then you'd miss out on the dramatic main room where the fun really begins.

I'm not usually a fan of tasting menus; they're always too long, showoffy, and dictatorial ("You vil eet zee veal bladder wit chocolate soos and you vil like eet!"). But here they do it right. Six savory courses are offered, all sized for enjoyment and concocted with genius. Ora king salmon gets the right amount of shock from lemon, dill, and horseradish, warm corn custard comes with langoustines and chorizo, and a loin of spring lamb gets a crispy lamb-neck garnish. The sauces are always superb (vin jaune on organic chicken, miso soubise on skirt steak, béarnaise on beef) and the salads are so artistic, you won't want to disturb them. Sweetbreads don't show up enough in restaurants for our taste, but here they're roasted reverentially (to juicy and still fork-tender) and served on white polenta with glazed bacon. A more satisfying thymus gland you will never encounter.

It's a testament to the excellence of Las Vegas restaurants that Sage is considered just another slugger in a lineup of great places to have dinner. It's not cheap, but it's so tasty you won't mind getting converted to the cult of Shawn McClain.

GET THIS

Bourbon; kusshi oysters with tequila mignonette; oxtail crostini; foie gras crème brûlée; hanger steak; roasted carrots; heirloom tomato salad; Hamachi crudo salad; ora king salmon; loin of spring lamb; veal cheeks; corn custard with langoustines; lamb belly; organic chicken with sauce vin jaune; roasted sweetbreads; slow-poached farm egg; whatever they're whipping up for dessert.

SPARROW + WOLF (WEST) American

see map 1, page 243
4480 Spring Mtn. Road, Suite 100
(702) 790 2147
sparrowandwolflv.com
Wed.-Mon., 5-11 p.m.
$25-$75

Sparrow + Wolf is sleek and small (60 seats) and smells of wood smoke—all indicia of the haute-eclectic-bistro cooking that has taken over America in the past decade. Gastronomades who wander the Earth in search of oases of ingenious edibles have already pitched their tents here. Intrepid gastronauts, addicted to traveling where no man has gone before, have been here since day one. Simple gastronomes who revel in chef-enhanced high-quality ingredients will not be disappointed, either. But if you're the type who finds Spring Mountain Road too challenging (both geographically and gastronomically) or if you're simply looking for a good plate of grub, the sledding might be a tad heavy.

This is not to damn the culinary musings of Chef Brian Howard with faint praise, but only to point out that there's a lot going on here, both in your glass and on your plate. "Simple" is not a word in Howard's vocabulary. With this long-awaited opening in the heart of Chinatown, he threw down a gauntlet among the pho parlors and noodle shops and immediately complicated non-Asians' relationship to this three-mile-long pan-Pacific island of culinary delights.

Just as complicated are the cocktails—at least five ingredients each—but they're as tasty as the food if you go for that sort of thing. The wine list matches the menu, the neighborhood, and the crowd, even if it doesn't match what a wine snob might want to drink.

Howard's good eats begin with his charcuterie platter: not yet made in-house, but top-quality stuff. Alongside these meats are seasonal pickles he does make on the premises and they're fabulous. Just as good are his oysters topped three different ways, with pineapple mignonette, cucumber granité, and a yuzu pearl. The Chinatown clams casino, baked with uni (sea urchin) hollandaise, is so rich it ought to come with its own calorie count, but it's also fusion food at its finest.

Like I said, nothing is simple; roasted beets come under a tangle of endive, pea shoots, shaved fennel, sheep's-milk blue cheese, and "bird seed" (black sesame seeds)! Quite a mouthful, but everything has its place. Butcher Wings with burnt-tomato 'nduja vinaigrette are one in a bevy of beautiful plates that dot the menu: beef-cheek with bone-marrow dumplings, sweetbreads with smoked bacon, firm toothsome halibut coated with Alabama white-barbecue sauce, and udon noodles "Bolognese" with Taggiasche olives, citrus confit, and mint. Octopus on top of a very good steak sounds contrived, but if you taste carefully and think a little harder, you see that a lot of consideration went into these combinations, and by and large they work. Nowhere is this payoff more rewarding than in his Campfire Duck, gorgeous slices of duck and foie gras resting on dark earthy shreds of wood-ear mushrooms, accented by sharp bites of salted plum in a duck-bone broth. It's a dish that appears to be trying to do too much, but those flavor explosions in your mouth tell you that it succeeds.

This is high-wire cooking without a net, and when Howard pulls it off, the results are thrilling indeed.

GET THIS

House-baked bread; oysters three ways; halibut with white Alabama BBQ sauce; Campfire Duck; Butcher Wings; Chinatown clams casino; udon "Bolognese"; beef-cheek and bone-marrow dumplings; charcuterie; sweetbreads with smoked bacon.

see map 1, page 243
5040 W. Spring Mtn. Road, #5
(702) 251-0022
nakamurayalv.com
11:45 a.m.-11 p.m., daily
$25-$75

Unique, tasty, and underrated are the three words I use to describe Kengo Nakamura's *wafuu* (Japanese-style) pastas at his namesake restaurant. What he whips up nightly is more interesting than 90% of the macaroni you find on the Strip and the biggest problem is trying to keep yourself from ordering half the menu.

For the uninitiated, *wafuu* is a type of small restaurant that substitutes Italian pasta for rice in many traditional Japanese dishes. Here you get choices like spaghetti with squid-ink sauce, pasta with crab and mentaiko (dried fish roe), miso carbonara, or fettucine tossed with tomato cream and kurobuta sausage. Kengo-san also heaps excellent seafood on capellini in one of his simpler dishes or tosses sea urchin with cream for one of his richer ones. He can wow you with his mochimugi (barley) risotto or a delicate shabu-shabu salad.

One of the problems with this place is the three different platforms to order off of. (This is a good problem to have.) You're confronted by a large blackboard to your left as you enter the small room, which contains the menu's greatest hits. Then, the multi-page printed menu is chock full of good-to-great things to eat. Finally, the helpful wait staff presents a specials blackboard at your table. Our advice: Get everything on the specials board and pick and choose a few items from the other two.

Three things you won't want to miss are the fried "Jidori" chicken, crispy dark meat with the thinnest of coatings, the piquant octopus (or kanpachi) carpaccio, and the mizuno salad tossed with a delicate dressing and well-chosen greens. That chicken shows up again in an irresistible "Takana" spaghetti (swimming in a light chicken broth), tasting like the perfect marriage of ramen and Rome. Italy is paid further homage in a red-white-green Italian "hamburg" covered in melted mozz on top of a fresh tomato sauce beside a bunch of broccoli. The pasta dishes possess a lightness you rarely find in American-Italians (although by Japanese standards, this food is a gut-bomb), but every dish is adroitly sized for sharing among up to four diners. A more than passable tiramisu tastes like it was made minutes earlier, rather than biding its time in the fridge for days.

Overseeing it all is Kengo-san, who presides over the dining room from behind his open-kitchen counter. The bilingual waitresses are very helpful and the beer and sake selections are perfectly matched to the food.

So many Japanese spots captivate us these days due to the carefulness of the cooking and the palpable passion behind the projects. All restaurants aim to make money, but Americans too often cook for the cash. The Japanese look upon restaurants as a calling.

GET THIS

Jidori chicken; house-baked bread; octopus kanpachi; mizuno salad; Italian "hamburg" steak; shabu-shabu salad; squid ink pasta; pasta with mentaiko; mochimugi risotto; miso carbonara; sea urchin pasta; mussels; "Takana" spaghetti; fettucine with tomato cream; tiramisu.

TWIST BY PIERRE GAGNAIRE (STRIP) French

Mandarin Oriental
at CityCenter
(888) 881-9367
mandarinoriental.com
Tues.-Sat., 6-10 p.m.
$75-$125

Like a few other restaurants in our Essential 52, Twist isn't for everyone. Like all restaurants in the Pierre Gagnaire oeuvre, it takes a decidedly adventuresome tack toward most of its menu, which consists mainly of riffs on ingredients presented in a blizzard of small plates. If you're looking for portion size or a standard three-course (app-main-dessert) dinner, look elsewhere. But if you're an intrepid epicure, you'll think you've died and gone to heaven. Which pretty much also describes the room, as heavenly and romantic a space (overlooking Aria and the Crystals Mall) as you'll find on the Strip.

Once you're seated, though, the fun really starts. It's impossible to get bored by Gagnaire's food. The menu changes seasonally and very few "standards" are on it, so whatever I rave about—be it shellfish mariniere with champagne herb sauce and black gnocchi or a trio of savory ice creams—might be long gone by the time you show up. Take heart. This former enfant terrible of French cuisine will capture your attention from the first array of amuse bouche through flights of oyster fancy, accented with everything from sardine rillettes and blue curaçao to frozen bananas. How does he think these things up? Who knows, but they invariably work and keep you smiling and guessing throughout the meal.

If you're saddled with a beef 'n' taters dining companion, don't despair. The steaks here are pricey, but meltingly tender and some

of the best in town. Does anyone on Earth make better veal tenderloin? Probably not. Ditto the Bordelaise and Béarnaise sauces. An avant-garde restaurant that also serves tremendous beef (and some of the most stunning vegetarian creations on the planet) sounds like an impossible balancing act, but the chefs here pull off this magic nightly with the consistency of stone masons. The wine list is smaller than those at other top-notch frog ponds, with lots of bottles that won't have you reaching for your heart medicine. When Twist opened in 2009, the wine list was one of the weaker things about it. These days it competes with any (wine) watering hole in town.

Things have gotten a bit more expensive here over the years, but the tasting menus are priced competitively with the likes of Le Cirque ($135-$180), rather than stratospherically like Savoy and Robuchon ($250-$450). Where its competitors feel more like churches of fine dining, Twist is where you go to have fun. French food conquered the world because of the discipline and deliciousness of its recipes. Twist conquered Las Vegas with a blend of perfection and whimsy. On any night of any season, I'll put a meal here up against any in the country.

GET THIS

Vegetarian tasting menu; Grand tasting menu; Pierre's salad; veal tenderloin; Zezette bouillon; Hudson Valley foie gras two ways; smoked haddock and scallop soufflé; Dover sole; wild European turbot; Maine lobster; Nebraska prime ribeye; Pierre's dessert medley.

URBAN TURBAN (EAST) Indian

see map 1, page 243
3900 Paradise Road
(702) 826-3217
urbanturbanvegas.com
11 a.m.-10:30 p.m., daily
$25-$75

Like any great restaurant town—New York, Chicago, Tokyo, etc.—Vegas is an edible orgy to an epicure. Lying before you are endless pleasures of the flesh: ripe, nubile, willing morsels there for the taking. But as anyone who's ever been to an orgy can tell you, it can also be exhausting and overwhelming … or so I've heard.

There's such a thing as too much of a great thing, be it an excess of Italian, an overflow of fine French, or a surfeit of steak. I can even overdose occasionally on superior sushi. When a confluence of greatness occurs, only one cuisine helps me re-calibrate my desires and regain my taste senses: Indian.

Indian food overwhelms the senses in a good way. It's plenty spicy, but not in the sense of extreme heat (although some Indian food can be fiery); rather, every dish contains Himalayan peaks of piquancy. Subtlety is not its strong suit. Kaleidoscopic flavors, intense aromas, and powerful punches to the palate define it. Only Cajun cooking marries less well with wine. But the depth and richness of its soups and stews are deeply soul-stirring. The Japanese may have defined umami, but Indian culture imbues its cuisine with

almost mystical levels of savory complexity.

A relative newcomer on the Vegas food scene, Urban Turban has tapped into the origins of this food and given it a modern spin unlike any other Indian you've probably ever encountered. Separating it from the pack are small bites and more creative plating than in your average Indian joint and food both more refined and polished than the stew and soup-centric stuff you usually get.

Credit for this goes to Chef Tarun Kapoor, who brings a more modern sensibility to this menu without sacrificing the multidimensional ka-pow that distinguishes this cuisine. The butter chicken royale employs cream cheese to take this ground-nut butter-cashew sauce to a different level and his clay-oven-roasted fruits are a thing of subtle beauty. You won't find a more life-changing vegetarian stew than Kapoor's take on black-lentil dal—a surpassingly complex dish for something that looks so simple. Eighteen hours of cooking blends the lentils, spices, and milk into a buttery mass of vegetarian decadence. One bite in and you might forswear meat altogether. Equally good is his parda biryani (bread-covered rice), a satisfying marriage of two ingredients not usually made for each other. But unlike most nuptials between two starched souls, no friction ensues. Instead, you'll find yourself reflexively dipping into the rice with your bread, then dipping the both of them into the cool raita or the nice warm tomato sauce on the side.

As I said at the top, few Western cuisines can match the depth of this food. Between the long slow cooking, the raft of spices, and the liberal use of legumes, you'll find yourself hardly missing meat at all. If you do, Kapoor has plenty of proteins to satisfy, like a traditional goat curry, banana-leaf fish, or his more modern tandoori tacos. Tuesdays, they put out a vegan buffet—pani puri potatoes, yellow-lentil stew, garlic-cup corn, vegetable-medley korma, sweet-mushroom garlic, and other compound-adjective dishes—that's so good, it will purge all those loathsome carnivorous cravings from your animal-murdering soul. Almost.

GET THIS

Turbanator salad; lentil cappuccino; samosa chat; vodka pani puri; lemon and herb vegetable skewers; tandoori chicken; tandoori tacos; lamb seekh; shrimp "my-way"; banana-leaf fish; goat curry; butter chicken royale; parda biryani; black-lentil dal; vegetable korma medley.

WING LEI (STRIP)

Chinese

Wynn Las Vegas
(702) 770-3388
wynnlasvegas.com
5:30-10 p.m., daily
$75-$125

Confucius said a man cannot be too careful about what he eats, but he obviously never came to Wing Lei—a place where you can just close your eyes and point and still be assured of eating the best Chinese food east of Shanghai. Not only is it our most elegant Chinese restaurant, but it's also one of the most elegant restaurants in all of Las Vegas, period.

From the smooth-as-Shantung-silk white-glove service and the best Peking duck in the business to garlic beef tenderloin of uncompromising tenderness, this is cuisine fit for a mandarin, especially those who like a little posh and circumstance with their Sichuan prawns. Lest you be someone who complains about paying premium prices for shrimp and stir-fries, keep in mind that the Chinese invented the whole shared-plates thing a couple of millennia ago—they just called it family-style—and it's the perfect way to keep portion and check sizes down.

And remember: These dishes are made with first-class groceries (unlike many a run-of-the-mill Chinese restaurant). Executive Chef Ming Yu doesn't know how to put out anything but an exquisite

plate of food, and his touch with Cantonese and Szechuan spicing is as graceful as the service. I'm not one for superlatives when it comes to steamed fish, but Yu's light touch with everything that swims takes us straight back to Hong Kong. High rollers from Asia (and we get lots of them) demand perfection in their stir-fries, nutty fried rice, and crispy General Tso's chicken, and Yu delivers it in spades. If you're a fan of any classic Chinese dish, from hand-pulled noodles to kung pao chicken, you'll feel like you're tasting these things the way they were meant to be made, not a version you're settling for in some past-its-prime Chinese dive.

There's nothing past its prime about the wine list, which is stocked with the usual big-hitter bottles for big-ego showoffs. The good news is the (relative) bargains to be found therein and the lower-priced nuggets are the ones that go perfectly with this food. Just look for anything German or Alsatian white, or ask the friendly somms for help.

As for desserts, they give lie to our usual advice about sweets in an Asian restaurant: If you want a good dessert in an Asian restaurant, go to a French one. No offense to Confucius, but the dude really could've learned something from diving into some sesame créme brûlée or a kalamansi cheesecake.

GET THIS

Peking duck; General Tso's chicken; steamed fish; garlic beef; seafood hot & sour soup; Alaskan geoduck clam; Dungeness crab (in season); Santa Barbara prawns; wok-tossed scallops; sampan prawns; mu shu pork; napa cabbage with Iberico ham; Yang Chow fried rice; desserts.

YUI EDOMAE SUSHI (WEST) Japanese

see map 1, page 243
3460 Arville Street Suite HS
(702) 202-2408
yuisushi.com
Mon.-Sat., 6-10:30 p.m.
$75-$125

Yui is obscure in location and impossible to see from the street – both of which lend just the right amount of Edomae (Tokyo-style) mystery to your experience. Don't be intimidated, though. If you're open to eating sushi the real way, which is to say the Japanese way, you will have the greatest raw-fish-eating experience in Las Vegas, and probably the best Wagyu beef-eating one as well.

Once you secure a reservation (definitely call ahead), you'll be greeted by the gracious and beautiful Tomoko-san, who will lead you past a sliding screen door into the land of serene sushi and sashimi so good, you'll think you're tasting these pristine fish for the first time. Just as terrific is the true, birth-certified, Japanese A-5 Wagyu, delicately grilled over white smokeless charcoal. No one puts a finer point on these things than the Land of the Rising Sun, and the nuances of flavor and texture can sometimes be subtle to the point of invisibility. But like all things exquisite, if you take the time to learn about them, you will be richly rewarded.

Where you'll reap these rewards will either be at the eight-seat sushi bar or one of the three booths facing the chefs (led by chef/

owner Gen Mizoguchi, the sushi master who put Kabuto on the map) as they work. Only two menus are offered: a nigiri tasting consisting of five courses (including 10 individual pieces of sushi) for $68, and an omakase ("chef's choice") menu for $120. The latter gets you those same 10 pieces of careful selected and sliced sushi (all of it sitting atop slightly warmed and carefully vinegared rice of almost unbelievable delicacy), along with appetizer, soup, sashimi, and grilled items. What shows up will be food of such beautiful simplicity that you may have to pinch yourself to remember that you're in Las Vegas. The rice is so perfect, you can count the grains in your mouth as you're eating it, and the fish—everything from baby sea bass to kamashita (collar) fatty tuna—is a revelation, and an education, in seafood. This is purist sushi for people who enjoy parsing the differences in texture between cuts of yellowtail, or those who go gaga over ikura (salmon roe) and kawahagi (leather blow fish).

The Japanese credo seems to be: Get out of the way and let the ingredient speak for itself. Seasonings and heat are always applied with a minimalist's touch, and whatever accents there are should, literally, barely touch the food. Thus do these chefs dedicate their lives to crafting each bite into something exquisite, a piece of food that creates a bond between the animal, the chef, and the customer. It's a bond that all chefs hope to achieve, but that Japanese chefs have turned into an art form. "Yui" roughly translates into that "unity between the chef and his diners," according to Gen-san. Put yourself in his hands and you'll feel the connection for yourself.

GET THIS

Nigiri sushi; omakase menu; Wagyu beef.

YUZU KAISEKI (WEST)

Japanese

see map 3, page 245
1310 E. Silverado Ranch Blvd.
(702) 778-8889
yuzukaiseki.com
Mon.-Thurs., 11:30 a.m.-2:30 p.m.;
5:30 p.m.-10 p.m.;
Fri.-Sat., 5 p.m.-1 a.m.
$25 or less

Yuzu may be small, but what it does is a very big deal, indeed. It's not strictly a sushi bar (although there is a small one), and it's not an izakaya in the Raku mold. Instead, it's our most Japanese of restaurants, a place that could be right at home in a Shinjuku alleyway—serving food so true to the rhythms and tastes of Japan that it's almost shocking when a *gaijin* walks through the door.

Among the many reasons to go here are the sushi, noodles, and teriyaki bowls, but if you really want to see chef-owner Kaoru Azeuchi strut his stuff, you need to reserve in advance for one of his kaiseki meals. For the uninitiated, *kaiseki* refers to a very specific form of Japanese dining. It's the haute cuisine of Japanese cooking—seasonal eating taken to the nth degree, a multi-course meal that combines the artistry of the chef with a myriad of ingredients, presentations, and techniques. Everything from the garnishes to the plating is thought through and presented in a way to enhance every sense—visual, aromatic, taste, even tactile—that goes into your enjoyment of the meal. Many of the elaborate garnishes are symbolic and all the recipes try to achieve a zen-like state of communion between the diner and the food.

Azeuchi trained for 16 years as a kaiseki chef in Japan, even getting the honor of serving the Emperor. Needless to say, you're in good hands.

A typical dinner might start with an appetizer platter containing

everything from an ethereal poached egg with caviar to grilled barracuda and uni rice topped with red snapper. From there, you proceed to a sashimi platter of lobster, striped jack, and halfbeak that's the equal of anything you'll find on the Strip or at Kabuto or Yui. Then comes the ultimate mushroom soup: a dobin-mushi matsutake broth containing pike conger, cabbage, and shrimp, so startling in its deceptive smoky simplicity that it will spoil you for soup forever.

The full Monty includes six more courses, ranging from grilled ribbons of A-5 Miyazaki Wagyu (wrapped around more 'shrooms and wasabi) and a steamed dish (steamed scallop cake draped with a latticework of wheat gluten) to eel tempura and a "vinegar dish" of seared mackerel that's a bracing combination of tart and smooth.

Like much Japanese food, once you stop looking for in-your-face flavor and start appreciating the nuances, you quickly find that you can't stop eating it. Here, you're treated to an education in the centuries-old traditions in the Land of the Rising Sun: the reverence for seafood, the harmony of vegetables, and the keen awareness of the seasons. In a nutshell, everything that Las Vegas is not. This is eating as a form of secular religion and if you're open to the experience, you'll be transported in a way that no other Western meal can match.

The kaiseki at Yuzu is not a formal affair, but because Kaoru-san flies in many ingredients from Japan, it's necessary to book at least three days in advance. How much you want to spend determines how elaborate it can be. The 10-course 16-dish affair we had runs about $175 per person, but for $50 each you can get a fine introduction to one of the greatest dinners in all of Las Vegas. Some of the simpler kaiseki dishes can be ordered a la carte as well if you just want to pop in for a quick bite and see what all the shouting is about. Don't miss the sake selection, either. It's the only thing to drink with this food.

GET THIS

Sushi, sashimi, teriyaki bowls; pork shouga yaki combo; chicken karaage combo; tempura special; sashimi special; chicken and egg bowl, yamakake bowl; udon noodles; homemade zaru tofu; housemade yuba (tofu skin); salmon aburi; tofu salad; poke salad; A5 Wagyu Japanese beef; black-pork shabu shabu; cold green-tea soba noodles; ramen nabe tonkotsu soy; dobin-mushi matsutake; kaiseki dinner.

TWIST

TOP TEN RESTAURANTS

Las Vegas is really two towns in one: the tourist corridor of downtown and the Strip, and off the Strip, where locals live and play.

Locals are famous for disdaining the Strip, and visitors rarely leave their comfortable hotels to go exploring the suburbs. Admittedly, 10 years ago, there wasn't much to explore, but these days, some top chefs in the neighborhoods can go turbot to turbot with anything the casinos are serving. And since locals are always asking me about my favorite off-Strip places, we thought it was high time to give credit to our burgeoning neighborhood restaurant scene and break out our Top Ten into two distinctive lists.

Also for the first time, I'm ranking the Top Ten according to my personal ratings of where to get the best experiences in food, service, and atmosphere. Obviously, these are highly subjective. The differences between the actual food on the plate at Twist versus Le Cirque, for instance, are so minuscule as to be almost undiscernible to all but the most trained palate. And then, after eating at these places back to back to back, even I get confused.

Still, on any night of the week, on average, in the following 20 restaurants, you'll have the best overall experience, taking into account everything from the view to the dessert wines.

Put another way, if the world's greatest gourmet came to town and asked me to take him/her on a month-long tour of the best restaurants on the Strip, these are the ones we'd hit, in order.

ON THE STRIP

Twist by Pierre Gagnaire
Joël Robuchon
Restaurant Guy Savoy
Le Cirque
L'Atelier de Joël Robuchon
Bazaar Meat
Sage
"e" by José Andrés
Carnevino
Carbone

OFF THE STRIP

Off-the-Strip restaurants are different animals entirely.

Gone are the casino money and thousands of customers funneling past your front door daily. Spending millions on décor and expecting a similar return on your dollar are out of the question. Instead, it's open on a shoestring and hang on for dear life. Out in the neighborhoods, it's sink or swim every day of the week and locally owned eateries struggle mightily against the currents of greedy landlords, clueless real estate developers, and character-less franchises.

No sane person would try to make a living feeding a public constantly racing to the bottom of the food trough (just look at all the cars parked in front of all-you-can-eat Asian buffets and Applebee's), but these operations are just crazy enough to buck those tides, as they try to upgrade what Las Vegans are eating. They deserve not only your business, but also a medal for making this town a much more civilized place in which to live. Here's my off-the-Strip list, in order.

Ferraro's Italian Restaurant and Wine Bar
Raku/Raku Sweets
Yui Edomae Sushi
Marché Bacchus
Andre's Bistro & Bar
Other Mama
Sparrow + Wolf
Elia Authentic Greek Taverna
EATT Gourmet Bistro
Carson Kitchen

BOTTOM 10

Do you enjoy overpriced tourist traps? Tired food? Dated décor? Handing over hard-earned money to celebrity chefs phoning it in?

Then Las Vegas has you covered!

This city boasts dozens of the world's greatest restaurants, but it also hosts more than a few half-baked concepts, licensing deals with

"name" chefs, and sad old war horses, and all exist solely to separate the uninformed and gullible from their cash.

Instead here are my selections for Vegas restaurants to avoid—and my reasons why.

10) Italian-American Club—An old saying goes, "The quality of an Italian restaurant is inversely proportional to the number of pictures of Frank Sinatra on the walls." There are *a lot* of pictures of Sinatra on these walls.

9) Leticia's—I used to love Leticia's; then again, I used to love my ex-wives.

8) SW Steakhouse—If you're the type who relishes wearing a dog collar while being verbally abused after gargling with razor blades as electric shocks are being applied to your genitals, you'll enjoy perusing this wine list, then paying the straight-up-your-fundament tariff.

7) Piero's—Squint real hard as you look at the crowd here and you'll still see bell-bottoms, bouffants, and muttonchops. The list of celebrities who have eaten here is legendary, almost as legendary as celebrities' ignorance about good food.

6) RM Seafood—Rick Moonen is an iconic chef who's forgotten more about seafood than I'll ever know. Unfortunately, his staff didn't get the memo that they were supposed to remember these things.

5) Battista's Hole in the Wall—Italian food served in buckets to the hoi polloi who love garlic, soggy noodles, and unlimited soda pop masquerading as house wine. The pictures on the wall are a nice distraction from food from which distraction is needed.

4) The Bootlegger—When you're ready to throw in the towel, and no longer give a shit, you go to the Bootlegger—strictly for those who wish Ronald Reagan was still in office, think of Nancy Reagan as a style icon, and refer to Wayne Newton as "The Kid."

3) Michael's—Do you think a palate-cleansing sorbet is the height of sophistication? Love rubbing shoulders with low-rent high rollers? Then you'll be in comped hog heaven here.

2) Masa—Heart-attack-priced sushi served in an airplane hangar that feels like a gymnasium, which you'll wish was a hospital when you get your bill.

1) Momofuku—A tsunami of umami, strictly for Millennials who think David Chang is a culinary god because he stuck some pork belly in a bao bun.

CAVIAR TACOS AT ROSE. RABBIT. LIE.

Section II

Additional Recommendations

OYSTERS AT IZAKAYA GO

Additional Recommendations Introduction

The second half of the book provides plentiful additional suggestions for Las Vegas' top restaurants in the many categories that readers, neighbors, colleagues, family, friends, and total strangers frequently ask us to recommend. Additionally, you'll find expanded sections on Chinatown, steakhouses, French restaurants, buffets, and burgers. Maps and a detailed index eliminate any challenge you might have for locating every eatery referenced in the book.

Note that Huntington Press (the publisher of the *Eating Las Vegas* series) also maintains LasVegasAdvisor.com, which covers the Las Vegas dining scene extensively. There you can find lengthy and constantly updated listings of cheap eats, local favorites, late-night dining spots, and additional meal options in more categories than appear here. And although I don't frequent the buffets, I have a huge amount of respect for the chefs who work in them and the customers who enjoy the ability to sample a lot of different food for one set price, and there had to be a buffet listing in this volume. Here again, input from the *Las Vegas Advisor* was paramount in identifying the city's best.

One quick word about locations. Each of the entries in this section includes an address and phone number. When a recommendation has two or three locations, it's noted, and when it has more than three, it's listed as "multiple locations." The address and phone for each are presented according to the following protocol. If there's an original or clearly dominant location, that's the one that's listed. And if not, the location that's geographically closest to the Strip is used. When a restaurant appears in more than one section, the location and phone are provided in the first listing only and subsequent listings refer back to the original.

SEAFOOD HOTPOT AT THE CHUBBY CATTLE

CHINATOWN

When Chinatown Plaza opened in 1995—housing five restaurants and a smattering of shops—Spring Mountain Road was known mainly for its potholes. No one thought of this area as Chinatown and it was audacious of the developers to call it such. Twenty-two years later, I estimate I've eaten in more than 110 restaurants along Spring Mountain Road. All you can do is applaud their prescience and marvel at what this three-mile stretch of road has become.

At last count, more than 120 Asian restaurants line this avenue (and, it seems, triple that number of massage parlors and nail salons). These days, the whole stretch of street from Valley View to Jones is a veritable buffet of Asian eats and it's a must-stop on any foodie tour of Las Vegas. Intrepid gastronauts know this is where you come to get the real deal in Chinese barbecue, Japanese noodles, and giant bowls of whatever soup suits your fancy—all at astoundingly cheap prices. For example, dinner for two at Zen Japanese Curry costs roughly what a glass of wine will run you at Wynn/Encore.

Sushi hounds also know that the fish you'll find at Kabuto and Yui is every bit the equal of what you get in the hotels, again at significantly lower prices, and nothing on the Strip competes with the plethora of Japanese izakaya and robatayaki parlors that have popped up in recent years, many open late and catering to the hungover and the about-to-be.

All told, Las Vegas' Chinatown is a treasure in its own right and the first thing I point to whenever some food snob from New York or San Francisco (they're always from New York or San Francisco) pooh-poohs our food culture as being an inorganic top-down product of too much casino money and too little taste. So grab your chopsticks and dive in.

Some notes about the following list. For the most part, these are places I highly recommend, although a few are noted not for endorsement, but because they're popular and pretty terrible, so I thought you should be forewarned. Almost every restaurant has been visited by me multiple times. Nevertheless, chefs and owners change sometimes without notice (you'll never see an "Under New Management" sign in an Asian restaurant), so occasionally, dropoffs in cooking quality (e.g., China Mama) occur with no warning.

Finally, none of these joints are for picky eaters. The whole point of eating along Spring Mountain Road is that it's the closest you'll ever get to the real thing without a 14-hour flight across the Pacific. In some of these places, English is definitely a second language. In others, service is, how you say, not of the most professional and friendly quality. But arrive with an open mind and adventuresome palate and you'll be an Asian maven in no time.

168 Market

3459 S. Jones Boulevard
(702) 363-5168

Full-service Asian grocery store, probably the best one of the bunch in Chinatown, with fresh fish and takeout galore.

Asian BBQ & Noodle

3400 S. Jones Boulevard #5C
(702) 202-3636

Go well before noon or mid-afternoon if you want to get a seat. Max Jacobson, one of the original authors of this book, endorsed this as the best Chinese barbecue in Vegas and I have no reason to argue with him. Closed Fridays. (Yes, Fridays. Oh, those crazy Asians.)

BBQ King

5650 Spring Mountain Road
(702) 364-8688

Cash only. Cantonese only.

Big Wong

5040 Spring Mountain Road #6
(702) 368-6808

Beef noodle soups to beat the band.

SALT AND PEPPER CHICKEN WINGS AT BIG WONG

Café Noodle & Chinese Barbecue
4355 Spring Mountain Road #104
(702) 220-3399

Another old reliable that still delivers the goods.

HOUSE LOBSTER SPECIAL AT CAPITAL SEAFOOD RESTAURANT

Capital Seafood Restaurant
4215 Spring Mountain Road
(702) 227-3588

In the original Chinatown Plaza, going strong for 20 years. Superb Cantonese lobster stir-fries at half the cost you'd pay a mile to the east.

Chengdu Taste (Essential 52: see page 50)

China Mama
3420 S. Jones Boulevard
(702) 873-1977

Still reliable, but the cooking quality has diminished over time and it's not the force it once was.

Chubby Cattle

3400 S. Jones Boulevard
(702) 868-8808

Conveyor-belt hot pot is the mode at this new Mongolian eatery. Some of it is hokey, but the extensive menu has legitimate—and sometimes esoteric—Asian surprises in store.

Crab Childe Yunnan Tasty Garden

5115 Spring Mountain Road
(702) 826-4888

The real deal. No one speaks English; you're surrounded by fellow travelers of all stripes, and (if you're a round-eye) they look at you like you're nuts when you walk through the door. (Expect a lot of "you no like" when you try to order.) Not for the timid, but really *really* good.

Harbor Palace Seafood

4275 Spring Mountain Road
(702) 253-1688

Another long-standing place that's a big hit with the tour-bus crowd. Haven't been in years, but with so many great newer places, I see no reason to return.

J&J Szechuan Cuisine

5700 Spring Mountain Road
(702) 876-5983

Our favorite, old-school, go-to Szechuan now has serious competition, but still shines.

SZECHUAN SPECIALTY AT J&J SZECHUAN CUISINE

Joyful House

4601 Spring Mountain Road
(702) 889-8881

One of those truly terrible places that's been around forever. Strictly for the sweet-and-sour-pork crowd.

Miàn Sichuan Noodle

4355 Spring Mountain Road
(702) 483-6531

Straight from the San Gabriel Valley comes this offshoot featuring the fiery mouth-numbing noodle soup/stews of Sichuan. Guaranteed you'll be the only haole in the joint.

Niu-Gu Noodle House

3400 S. Jones Boulevard #16
(702) 570-6363

Limited menu, gorgeous presentation, wonderful whole fish, and oh! Those noodles. You won't be able to stop slurping.

Ping Pang Pong (Gold Coast Casino)

(702) 367-7111

It's not really in Chinatown. But it's nearby and serves some of the best dim sum in town. Unfortunately, you have to brave the environs of the Gold Coast to get to it, and go early: By noon every day, the place is full of Asians and Caucasians fighting for a table.

SUSHI AT PING PANG PONG

Sam Woo BBQ

4215 Spring Mountain Road B101
(702) 368-7628

About every other year, this joint gets closed down for a day or two for health-code violations. "So what?" I say. "And when the sun comes up in the morning, does it catch you unawares?"

Shang Artisan Noodle

4983 W. Flamingo Road
(702) 888-3292

Dinner and a show! Or lunch and a cooking lesson. No matter when you arrive, they'll be hand-pulling noodles in that wonderful piece of sleight-of-hand that makes for delicious Chinese lamian. Don't miss the spicy wontons or the beef pancake.

The Noodle Man

6870 S. Rainbow Boulevard
(702) 823-3333

Not strictly in Chinatown, but wonderful hand-pulled ribbons are thrown and cut out in the open (they make a show out of it). Noodle Man is a southwest Vegas favorite for its delicious soups and other noodle-based dishes.

Veggie House

5115 Spring Mountain Road #203
(702) 431-5802

A full menu of classic Chinese dishes and some not-so-classic house specials (try the crispy spicy eggplant), all using vegetarian ingredients only. Open for lunch and dinner, dine in or take out.

Wendy's Noodle Café

3401 S. Jones Boulevard
(702) 889-3288

Sort of an all-purpose Taiwanese café with pleasant service and an easy-to-navigate menu. A good place to get your feet wet if you're new to this food.

BEEF NOODLE SOUP AT SHANG ARTISAN NOODLE

GO!KU J-Wraps & Ramen

4300 Spring Mountain Road
(702) 998-9781

Not in the same league as Monta and Ramen Sora, but a good alternative when those are packed.

J-WRAP PLATTER AT GO!KU J-WRAPS & RAMEN

Hachi Japanese Yakitori Izakaya

3410 S. Jones Boulevard
(702) 227-9300

Another newcomer to our izakaya revolution, Hachi is well-run and more inventive than most.

Izakaya Go

3775 Spring Mountain Road
(702) 247-1183

Sake houses have been popping up like cherry blossoms in April lately, and this is one of the best. The menu is huge, the fish impeccable, and the robatayaki remarkable.

Japanese Curry Zen

5020 Spring Mountain Road #1
(702) 985-1192

If price to value were the only criterion, Zen would beat out Guy Savoy and Joël Robuchon for the best in town. Good gyoza, great spinach curry, insanely cheap prices.

Kabuto (Essential 52: see page 80)

Monta Ramen

5030 Spring Mountain Road
(702) 367-4600

Still the gold standard for authentic ramen in Vegas, this extremely popular nook pretty much started Chinatown on its upswing. The dashi (or broth) is supple and sublime. Get there early, as it packs in a crowd regularly, even though it's no longer the only noodle shogun in town.

Raku/Sweets Raku (Essential 52: see page 108)

Ramen KoBo

7040 S. Durango Drive
(702) 489-7788

The owners of perennial-favorite Monta are making their own noodles in this suburban location. The excellent dashi-filled bowls are much spicier here than at the mother restaurant. Konichi-yowza!

TSUKEMEN AT RAMEN KOBO

Ramen Sora

4490 Spring Mountain Road
(702) 685-1011

Sapporo ramen—rich, nutty, and sweet—is perfect for a cold day in the desert. Monta's broth may be more refined, but Ramen Sora fills the bill any season (but summer).

Ramen Tatsu

3400 S. Jones Boulevard
(702) 629-7777

Another ramen joint that will do in a pinch when the two superstars, Monta and Ramen Sora, are full.

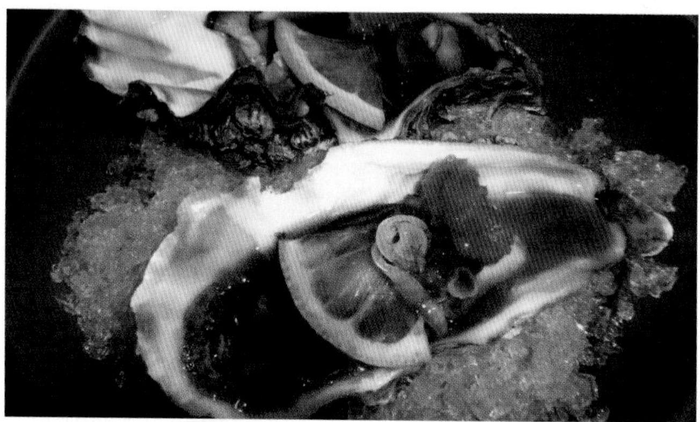

OYSTERS IN PANZU SAUCE AT SAKE HOUSE ICHIZA

Sake House Ichiza

4355 Spring Mountain Road #205
(702) 367-3151

A grimy second-floor joint that's seen better days, but the food is pretty nifty.

Trattoria Nakamura-Ya (Essential 52: see page 118)

Wafuu pasta, a Japanese take on Italian food, is the specialty here and dish after dish is fascinating and fun. Order off the big chalkboard and expect some of the most interesting food in town.

Udon Monzo

3889 Spring Mountain Road
(702) 202-1177

Ramen is everywhere in Chinatown; it's time it got a little competition from these thick, chewy, rectangular, and soft wheat-starch noodles from Marugame, Japan. At peak hours, you'll have to wait in line. It's worth it.

Yui Edomae Sushi (Essential 52: see page 126)

8oz Korean Steakhouse & Bar

4545 Spring Mountain Road B #105
(702)909-3121

The newest entrant in our upgraded Korean meat sweepstakes is also the best. The name comes from the larger portion sizes here versus what gets served in Seoul. Me thinks even Kim Jong Un would approve. Cool bar, too.

Hobak Korean BBQ

5808 Spring Mountain Road #101
(702) 257-1526

Korean 'cue took a big leap forward in the past year and this cacophonous casual spot led the way with better beef and upgraded banchan. If only they'd turn the music down.

Honey Pig (2 locations)

4725 Spring Mountain Road K / 9550 S. Eastern Avenue #100
(702) 876-8308 / (702) 979-9719

Panchan cooking at its finest. Which means you do all the work on an inverted wok, holding everything from all of those obscure cuts of Korean beef to the last squid standing. Come with a crowd and you'll enjoy yourself. Come as a deuce and you'll wonder what hit you.

KOREAN BARBECUE AT HONEY PIG

MOTHER'S KOREAN GRILL

Kkulmat Korean Kitchen

5600 Spring Mountain Road Suite A
(702) 333-4845

Koreans love to show you pictures of their food on the menu and throughout the restaurant. We gringos appreciate the photos and the food. Pilgrims from both sides of the Pacific will love this simple homey fare without all the choreography you find in Korean steakhouses.

Lee's Korean BBQ

6820 Spring Mountain Road
(702) 388-0488

Mr. Lee (owner of a local chain of liquor stores more known for quantity than quality) owns this joint as well and highly recommends it! Or at least that's what the billboards all around town say. Personally, as soon as we see an "all-you-can-eat" sign, we turn the car around.

Magal BBQ

4240 Spring Mountain Road
(702) 476-8833

Of all our new, higher-toned, franchise, Korean BBQ joints, this one has the most Seoul. (Sorry.)

Mother's Korean Grill

4215 Spring Mountain Road #107
(702) 579-4745

My go-to spot for dolsot bimbimbap and other Korean standards. Not spectacular, but friendly and consistent, unlike some other Korean joints that seem to change ownership more often than I do my socks.

Tofu Hut

3920 Spring Mountain Road
(702) 257-0072

Good cheap bowls of Korean soups that all taste alike to me.

YuXiang Korean-Chinese Cuisine

7729 S. Rainbow Blvd. Ste 3
(702) 790-3474

Korean-Chinese food is a thing, and it's a thing that's finally come to Las Vegas. The noodles are thick, the sauces are practically black, and the crispy beef is out of this world. Don't miss the jjajangmyeon.

KUNG PAO SHRIMP AT YUXIANG KOREAN-CHINESE CUISINE

Chuchote Thai Bistro & Dessert

4105 W. Sahara Ave.
(702) 685-7433

Our newest entry in our Thai One On universe is a classy little joint with upscale dishes and a take-no-prisoners southern Thai vibe. The desserts are frozen and inventive and you'll need them to quell the heat.

CHU CHEE CRISPY PRAWN AT CHADA THAI AND WINE

Chada Street/Chada Thai (Essential 52: see page 48)

Krung Siam Thai

3755 Spring Mountain Road #102
(702) 735-9485

Old-fashioned Thai. Great lunch special.

Kung Fu Thai & Chinese Restaurant

3505 S. Valley View Boulevard
(702) 247-4120

The granddaddy of Thai restaurants in town. It still does that over-sweet-thing that American Thai restaurants can't get away from, but it's a solid choice, and the yen ta foe (pink noodle soup) is pretty darn scrumptious.

Ocha Thai

1201 S. Las Vegas Blvd.
(702) 386-8631

Traditional Thai a cut or three above all that gloppy sweet stuff you find in the 'burbs. Since 1989, Ocha has been holding down the fort downtown for lovers of the real deal in moo dad deaw (pork jerky) and tod mun (fish cake).

Weera Thai

3839 W. Sahara Avenue #9
(702) 873-8749

It's not technically in Chinatown, which is a couple of miles north, but Weera rates a major wave for its northern Thai specialties, regional variety—Laos and Issan are represented—and beautifully crafted duck dishes.

Vietnamese

No matter how much I try to discern the differences in this or that pho (or the menus, for that matter), I never can. So, rather than strain my brain attempting to differentiate among these places, all I can do is vouch for them. All of these are good, if remarkably similar. District One is great.

District One (Essential 52: see page 56)

LOBSTER NOODLE BROTH AT DISTRICT ONE

Pho 87
3620 S. Jones Boulevard
(702) 233-8787

Pho Aimie
8390 S. Rainbow Blvd.
(702) 776-7017

Pho Kim Long
4029 Spring Mountain Road
(702) 220-3613

THAI 2 AT PHO SAIGON #8

Pho Saigon #8
9055 S. Eastern Avenue #1C
(702) 629-3100

Pho Sing Sing
2550 S. Rainbow Boulevard
(702) 380-2999

Pho Vietnam
4215 Spring Mountain Road B201
(702) 227-8618

Viet Noodle Bar
5288 Spring Mountain Road #106
(702) 750-9898

Fiesta Filipina

3310 S. Jones Boulevard
(702) 252-0664

Try as I might, I've never enjoyed a single bite of food in a Filipino restaurant. Much like Greek, home cooking is where you'll find the best of this country's cuisine. But if you insist, knock yourself out. The lumpia are less greasy than usual here, but the fish is as overcooked as ever.

Halal Guys

3755 Spring Mountain Road #101
(702) 889-6123

Get in line with the cheap-eats crowd and expect to be underwhelmed by what gets slopped onto your plate.

COMBO PLATE AT HALAL GUYS

Hawaiian Style Poke

3524 Wynn Road
(702) 202-0729

All poke, all the time. Mixed daily. Usually half-a-dozen selections.

Island Malaysian Cuisine

5115 Spring Mountain Road
(702) 898-3388

COCONUT FRIED RICE WITH SHRIMP AND CHICKEN AT ISLAND MALAYSIAN CUISINE

This restaurant replaced another identical Malaysian restaurant that replaced an earlier restaurant that was indistinguishable from this one. And that pretty much tells you all you need to know about Malaysian restaurants in Las Vegas.

Pokeman

3735 Spring Mountain Road #206
(702) 550-6466

If bowls of rice and a boatload of sushi burritos float your boat, have at it.

Chinatown Desserts

With French, Italian, Mexican, Mediterranean, even American desserts available everywhere, why mess around with Asian? But if you must, all of these do that shaved-ice boba-tea thing Asian teenagers are so crazy about.

GREEN TEA CAKE AT CROWN BAKERY

Crown Bakery

4355 Spring Mountain Road #207
(702) 873-9805

Korean bakeries are a mystery to me. They love to make all sorts of French-sounding stuff puffed up into white-bread cakey concoctions almost identical in texture to one another. Plus, they do that bean-paste thing that's almost indefensible. (The Japanese and Chinese are guilty of this dessert misdemeanor as well.) That said, I always enjoy going to the Crown for some coffee and a pastry. Go figure.

Kung Fu Tea

5030 Spring Mountain Road
(702) 776-7077

Ronald's Donuts

4600 Spring Mountain Road
(702) 873-1032

A family-owned Las Vegas donut institution. The top two shelves are 100% vegan (actually approved by PETA).

SHAVED SNOW AND FRUIT AT SNOWFLAKE SHAVERY

Snowflake Shavery

5020 Spring Mountain Road
(702) 333-2803

Sunville Bakery

4053 Spring Mountain Road
(702) 889-9887

Supersoft and spongy breads, just the way the customers want them!

Tea Station

4355 Spring Mountain Road
(702) 889-9989

Volcano Tea House

4215 Spring Mountain Road 106B
(702) 207-7414

SKIRT STEAK AT STK

HIGH STEAKS: THE BEST BEEF IN VEGAS

How do you judge a steakhouse?

Is it the quality of the beef? How well they age it? Cook it? The variety of the side dishes? Or is it all about the wine list to you? Or the décor—dark, masculine, and clubby, or light, bright, and more modern? Maybe you demand tenderness at all costs? (For the record: a big mistake, since a superior, intensely mineral-rich, roasted-to-exquisite-beefiness strip sirloin should have a fair amount of chew to it.)

Maybe you're service-obsessive. Many people are. For them, the warmth of the welcome and speediness of the staff keep them coming back.

Perhaps you're a sucker for big bones. Or the type that occasionally gets a hankering for a (less expensive) hanger steak. Or someone who prefers cuts served in less traditional ways. Or likes a lot of folderol with their cholesterol.

Whoever you are, it's a fair bet that you're a conspicuous carnivore and nothing gets your juices flowing like tucking into a haunch of well-marbled steer muscle. If that sounds up your alley, you might consider moving to Las Vegas. Because next to the Big Apple, no city on Earth has better steakhouses than Sin City. And on any given night, I'll put our chef-driven joints up against anything New York City can throw at us.

True, for sheer volume, historical precedent, and breadth of menu options, nothing beats what you find in NYC, but if you look at many Big Apple classics, you'll find a number that haven't changed a thing on their menu in decades. If you close your eyes when you walk into Peter Luger, Keen's, Spark's, Wolfgang's, Gallagher's, Palm Too, and others, then gaze only at your plate, you won't be able to tell whether you're in 1978, 1998, or 2018. Yes, the steaks are magnificent and there's no replacing the testosterone-charged atmosphere in any of them, but in many ways, you're eating in a museum.

Not so in present-day Las Vegas, where the massive meat emporia give the chefs a lot of latitude to play with their food. These days, seasonal sides are all the rage and chefs like Matthew Hurley (CUT), Robert Moore (Prime), Sean Griffin (Jean-Georges), Ronnie Rainwater (Delmonico), Nicole Brisson (Carnevino), and David Thomas (Bazaar Meat) make things interesting from season to season, with a plethora of veggies, seafood, and other succulents that can keep even the fussiest gastronome unbored and happy.

Not only that, but between Carnevino's aging program and Bazaar Meat's over-the-top Spanish flair (not to mention that every top house in Vegas now features mind-blowing dry-aged steaks and multiple A-4 and A-5 cuts from Japan), we leave previously preeminent beef bastions like Chicago, Dallas, and Miami running in third, fourth, and fifth places. And if you do that eye-closing plate-gazing thing again, you can't tell the difference between the best of our beef and anything you bite into in midtown Manhattan.

None of these great steaks come cheap. Expect to pay $60+ for a pristine piece of prime, but face it, folks: We all eat too much cow now, so splitting one of these well-trimmed beauties (among two to four people) is the way to go.

No matter what your criteria, you can be assured that your steak might be the best you've ever had and that everything from the taters and foie gras to the desserts will have you dropping your fork in appreciation.

The Top 10 Steakhouses

Bazaar Meat (Essential 52: see page 32)

RIBEYE AT BAZAAR MEAT

Carnevino (Essential 52: see page 44)

CUT (Essential 52: see page 54)

NEW YORK STRIP AT DELMONICO STEAKHOUSE

Delmonico Steakhouse (Venetian)

(702) 414-3737

Like a few other time-worn and treasured Las Vegas restaurants, Delmonico has been around so long we tend to take it for granted. But like Emeril's, this venerable spot is due for a salute. It opened on May 3, 1999, and for nearly 18 years has been rendering drop-dead delicious versions of the food that made Emeril Lagasse famous.

Some people call it a steakhouse, but that doesn't tell half the story. I'd argue that, on any given night, the seafood here is every bit the equal of what's served by its big sister in the MGM Grand. I'd also argue that the gumbo is a dead ringer for the Bam Man's fare in N'Awlins itself and that the lobster bisque and crispy fried oysters are as good as you'll find 1,000 miles from the Gulf of Mexico. Of course, the steaks are first-rate too—especially the Nebraska-bred Piedmontese strip and the dry-aged cuts—but Executive Chef Ronnie Rainwaters' apple-cured, applewood-smoked, bone-in bacon and one of the best Caesar salads in the business have us licking our chops every time we walk in the place.

STRIP HOUSE DINING ROOM IN PLANET HOLLYWOOD

Gordon Ramsay Steak (Paris Las Vegas)

(702) 946-4663

Every restaurant in Vegas would be a steakhouse if it could be, and Ramsay, one of the best classical chefs in the business, was smart to recognize that fact. This, and his excellent burger joint at Planet Hollywood, keep him waist deep in pounds sterling, but be forewarned, not all Gordon Ramsay restaurants in Vegas are created equal. Mr. Profanity lent his name, but none of his talent, to the Gordon Ramsay Pub & Grill in Caesars. Stick with his steakhouse and burger palace if you want to retain a modicum of respect for what he once was.

MB Steak (Hard Rock)

(702) 483-4888

There hasn't been a Morton associated with the Morton's steakhouse brand since 1989. Whatever caché that chain once had was cashed in a long time ago. Founder Arnie Morton isn't around anymore, either, but his two sons have conspired to do his legacy proud with a cozy little corner of the Hard Rock Hotel that seamlessly blends new school and old. MB (Morton Brothers) Steak represents a definite upgrade from the previous meat emporium on the premises and the entrées and appetizers can dance beef cheek to beef cheek with any cholesterol-fest on the Strip, all at prices a bit softer than those in the big hotels. The wine list is a treat also—designed to get you drinking, not reaching for a respirator.

Prime (Essential 52: see page 106)

Strip House (Planet Hollywood)

(702) 737-5200

Sexy décor, sexy drinks, and sexy steaks. 'Tis a pity no locals ever come here, but it's understandable: The location is in a corner of PH so inconvenient that it takes a map and a Sherpa guide to find it. As it is, it's a big hit with middle managers and soccer moms thrilled to be seeing Britney Spears, few of whom have a clue about the great food they're getting.

Honorable Mention

Circus Circus Steakhouse (if you can stand the hotel), Lawry's The Prime Rib (an old standby that still delivers), Charlie Palmer Steak (a recent upgrade has got this place humming again), Hank's Fine Steaks (if you can stand driving to Henderson), Oscar's Steakhouse (the food has improved and you can't beat the décor, or the booze), and Tender (great game in season, if you can stand the hotel).

CIRCUS CIRCUS STEAKHOUSE

Bargain Steaks

Las Vegas is famous for its bargain steak and prime rib dinners, many of which run off and on as promotions in the casinos. The following are ongoing best bets for finding a good steak for under $20: Ellis Island, Herbs & Rye, Hitchin' Post Saloon and Steakhouse, Irene's, Jackson's Bar & Grill, and Rincon de Buenos Aires.

STEAK DINNER AT ELLIS ISLAND

EIFFEL TOWER RESTAURANT

FRENCH

Las Vegas is blessed with more great French food than anywhere in America that isn't New York City. The food our French chefs turn out every day, be it in a restaurant, brasserie, or bistro, tastes like you're a stone's throw from the Champs-Élysées. We had our own little French Revolution here (2005-2010), which saw names like Robuchon, Boulud, Gagnaire, and Savoy plant their flags on these desert shores and their standards of excellence continue to be the bar by which all chefs measure themselves.

André's (Essential 52: see page 28)

Bardot Brasserie (Essential 52: see page 30)

Bouchon (Essential 52: see page 40)

Café Breizh

3555 S. Fort Apache Rd.
(702) 209-3472

Small, but exquisite. A limited selection of croissant, tarts, crêpes, and brioche doesn't keep these from being the best you'll find this far from the Left Bank.

Delices Gourmands French Bakery

3620 W. Sahara Avenue
(702) 331-2526

A couple of miles west of the Strip in a strip mall that's seen better days, you'll find one of our better bakeries. Not much on décor, but the breads are très *fantastique* and the crêpes, huge baguette sandwiches, and canelés de Bordeaux are the genuine articles.

BREADS AT DELICES GOURMANDS FRANCH BAKERY

Additional Recommendations

EATT Gourmet Bistro
(Essential 52: see page 60)

LAMB WELLINGTON AT EATT HEALTHY FOOD

Eiffel Tower Restaurant
(Paris Las Vegas)
(702) 948-6937

They probably do more weddings here than in all other Vegas restaurants combined. Solid (if unimaginative) French fare amidst one of the most dramatic settings at which you will ever swoon over a soufflé.

Joël Robuchon (Essential 52: see page 76)

L'Atelier de Joël Robuchon (Essential 52: see page 84)

Le Cirque (Essential 52: see page 88)

Marché Bacchus (Essential 52: see page 94)

Mon Ami Gabi (Paris Las Vegas)
(702) 944-4224

Best people-watching in town (on the patio); best three-meals-a day French restaurant in town.

MON ABI GABI PATIO SEATING IN PARIS LAS VEGAS

Patisserie Manon

751 W. Charleston Boulevard #110
(702) 586-2666

Popular west-side neighborhood spot on the cusp of Summerlin. It doesn't hold a candle to Rosallie or Bouchon, but its macaroons and quiches will do in a pinch.

Picasso (Essential 52: see page 104)

Restaurant Guy Savoy (Essential 52: see page 110)

ALMOND CROISSANT AT ROSALLIE LE FRENCH CAFÉ

Rosallie Le French Café (Essential 52: see page 112)

Awesome pastries. Superb quiches. Serious coffee. The only thing I don't like about Rosallie is how far it is from my house.

Suzuya Pastries & Crepes

7225 S. Durango Drive #101
(702) 432-1990

Remarkable pastries in the southwestern part of town.

Twist (Essential 52: see page 120)

Wicked Spoon

BUFFETS

Las Vegas has been the Buffet Capital of the World for more than 70 years (since 1946 when the Buckaroo Buffet, Vegas' first midnight "chuckwagon," appeared at the El Rancho Vegas). Why do visitors and locals flock to them like lemmings to a cliff? Well, this city is synonymous with excesses—24-hour gambling, drinking, carousing, and eating. Yet while not every visitor is inclined to dive headlong into blackjack, booze, and all-night blowouts, culinary greed has never seemed tangled in moral issues.

If you're looking for quantity over quality and you're okay with starchy sauces over mystery meat and fish, gloppy casseroles, and salads that come from 55-gallon drums, just head for the cheapest buffet you can find. Still, some of the less expensive spreads are, actually, recommendable. Arizona Charlie's Decatur was revamped a couple of years ago and has a three-meal made-to-order grill; Main Street Station is the best and biggest buffet downtown; Station Casinos' Feast Buffets win on a price-to-quality comparison and extend good discounts with the players card; and Aliante, which started out as a Feast, is wildly popular with the north-valley locals and has a whole pig roast on Tuesdays.

However, the best buffets do tend to be the most expensive. Here they are.

Bacchanal Buffet (Caesars Palace)

(702) 731-7298

Ultra-modern 600-seat room with a reported 500 selections in nine different cuisines. It's so popular, even at the price, that they sell line passes for a mere $25 per person to people who want to avoid the long waits (the only line-pass-for-a-price buffet we know of). The seafood station is the most varied and high-quality in town.

THE BUFFET IN ARIA

The Buffet (Aria)

(702) 590-8630

Located on the second floor above the casino, this is one of the greatest gourmet buffets in Las Vegas and the least expensive among them (Cosmopolitan, Caesars, Wynn, and Bellagio); Bellagio is cheaper for breakfast. Everything served here is top-notch; the tandoori oven is unique to Vegas buffets (chicken, kabobs, naan) and the mozzarella bar is a great touch. The room is bright and clean; the service is exactly what you'd expect from such an upscale operation.

The Buffet (Bellagio)

(702) 693-8111

The Buffet at Bellagio made a big splash when it opened in 1996 and hasn't missed a beat since. You can count on the food being high-quality and it's the only buffet in town with a chef's table with a specialty menu that uses the freshest seasonal products. And there's a little bar play: Walk past the epic lines waiting to get in and see if there are any seats at the bar. If so, claim them! You pay the bartender at the end of the meal and your drinks are always right there.

The Buffet (Wynn Las Vegas)

(702) 770-3340

This buffet competes for best in Vegas. Fifteen action stations, including a whole rotisserie wall, a first-of-its-kind-in-North-America *parrilla* (grill), a chocolate fountain in which bakers dip an assortment of sweets, Frank Sinatra's family recipe for spaghetti and meatballs, plus short ribs, roast lamb, duck-leg cassoulet, and dim sum, Steve Wynn's own favorite food. It also caters to vegetarian/vegan, gluten-free, and diabetic diets.

Studio B (M Resort)

(702) 797-1000

M puts out a huge selection of more than 200 items and everything is restocked immediately. With the hordes of hungry this buffet attracts, how they keep up with it is a constant wonderment. Best of all, the prices are low for such a high-end spread. Only the Friday night seafood dinner is up there with the best gourmet superbuffets on the Strip. And *they* don't include unlimited beer and wine in the price.

Wicked Spoon (Cosmopolitan)

(702) 698-7870

With more than 11,000 reviews on Yelp and Trip Advisor averaging four stars, this buffet is obviously a standout. It also receives a number of editor's picks as best buffet in Las Vegas. Many selections come in individual portions in little bowls and pots, so you don›t have to scoop anything yourself, overload your plate, or overeat any one item. That said, the prime rib cuts and cracked king crab legs are big and abundant. One unusual carving-station item is the roasted bone marrow (reportedly super good for you). Definitely save room for dessert; the choices are too many to list and too good for spoiler alerts. And try the express take-out: $25 to load a container with as much as you can (the 2-for-1 coupon works here too).

THE BUFFET IN WYNN LAS VEGAS

BLACK ANGUS REUBEN AT BURGER BAR

BURGERS

Bachi Burger (multiple locations)

bachiburger.com

Unusual, innovative, and now at both ends of town.

Bobby's Burger Palace (The Shops at Crystals)

(702) 598-0191

Bobby Flay's burgers trump anything he's doing at Mesa Grill, although the burger there is also one of Vegas' best.

Burger Bar (Mandalay Place)

(702) 632-9364

Hubert Keller was the first fancy chef to bring a burger concept to Las Vegas and his are still some of the best.

Carnevino (Essential 52: see page 44)

Awesome meat. Awesome burger.

Carson Kitchen (Essential 52: see page 46)

Kerry Simon's butter burger is a legacy that does his memory proud.

BUTTER BURGER AT CARSON KITCHEN

CUT (Essential 52: see page 54)

Get the sliders at the bar.

Delmonico (see page 161)

Unlike most steakhouses (Carnevino being the exception), it's open for lunch and the burger is the thing to get with a nice glass of vin rouge.

Fatburger (multiple locations)

6775 W. Flamingo Road
(702) 889-9009

Next to Smashburger, this is my favorite franchised meat patty on a bun.

Fat Choy Restaurant (Eureka Casino)

(702) 794-0829

Sheridan Su's fusion burger is a piled-high delight.

FAT CHOY BURGER

Fleur by Hubert Keller (Mandalay Place)

(702) 632-9400

When a fine French chef does a bison burger like this one, we pay attention.

Fukuburger

3429 S. Jones Boulevard
(702) 262-6995

They put everything but the kitchen sink on these pan-Pacific patties, and if that's your thing, have at it.

Gordon Ramsay BurGR (Planet Hollywood)

(702) 785-5462

This is actually our favorite of the bombastic Brit's four Vegas eateries. And shhhhhh ... don't tell anyone, but the hot dogs are just as good as the burgers.

GOLD STANDARD BURGER AT HOLSTEINS SHAKES AND BUNS

Holsteins Shakes and Buns (Cosmopolitan)

(702) 698-7940

Perfect for when your nightclub buzz is wearing off at the Cosmo.

In-N-Out Burger (multiple locations)

4888 Dean Martin Drive
(702) 768-1000

Classics never go out of style. Nor does this "secret menu." Do you get yours "animal style"?

Marché Bacchus (Essential 52: see page 94)

A serious burger in a stunning setting.

Shake Shack (multiple locations)

New York-New York
(725) 222-6730

Danny Meyer took this concept public to great acclaim ... on Wall Street, no less. Aficionados know his is but a tepid ode to In-N-Out, at a substantially higher price. Still, people line up for them, so who are we to argue?

Smashburger (multiple locations)
smashburger.com

Everything is made fresh, so it's slower than fast-food usual, but the taste is worth the wait. Avoid the Caesars' food court Smashburger, whose prices are too dear.

Steak & Shake (South Point)
(702) 796-7111

I've been eating Steak & Shake burgers since I was six. These new franchises try to re-capture the glory of smashed grilled burgers, skinny fries, and Chili Macs from the '60s, but lack the proper seasoning that comes with great memories.

Stripburger (Fashion Show Mall)
(702) 737-8747

Decent burgers and shakes; great people-watching.

Umami Burger and Beer Garden (SLS Las Vegas)
(702) 761-7614

The burger that Los Angeles made famous is now in one of our best sports bars.

White Castle (Casino Royale)
(702) 227-8531

The original sliders are now on the Strip, muting the munchies and helping to halt hangovers at 4 a.m.

WHITE CASTLE BURGERS IN CASINO ROYALE

DESSERTS

ACE Donuts

9435 W. Tropicana Avenue
(702) 222-3370

Family owned and operated and completely fantastic.

Allegro (Essential 52: see page 26)

Leave the gun, eat the cannoli!

DONUT BREAD PUDDING AT CARSON KITCHEN

Carson Kitchen (Essential 52: see page 46)

The desserts change seasonally and never more than a few are on the menu, but your table will be fighting for the last bite.

Chef Flemming's Bake Shop

7 S. Water Street B & C, Henderson
(702) 566-6500

There are precious few reasons ever to venture to downtown Henderson, least of all to eat, but this little shop is a gem and worth the journey.

Delmonico (see page 161)

Steakhouse dessert used to be nothing but cheesecake and peach melba. Not so at Delmonico, where Diane Wong knows how to keep purists and fussy foodies alike satisfied.

Gelatology

7910 S. Rainbow Boulevard #110
(702) 914-9144

Desyree Alberganti's inventive gelatos are worth finding. Spoon-suckingly awesome, it's by far the best gelato in town. (And that includes all the fancy restaurants in all the fancy hotels.)

HEXX RETAIL STORE IN PARIS LAS VEGAS

Hexx Kitchen + Bar (Paris Las Vegas)

(702) 331-5100

Carol Garcia does bean-to-bar chocolate on a par with anything you'll find on either coast, and the rest of her sweets and shakes ain't too shabby either.

Lulu's Bread & Breakfast

6720 Sky Point Drive
(702) 437-5858

Big, fat, flaky, fruity pastries on the north side of town, with some interesting fresh-baked breads to take home with you, too.

Luv-It Frozen Custard

505 E. Oakey Boulevard
(702) 384-6452

An original slice (or cup, as it were) of Las Vegas' sweet side. A must-do.

Mothership Coffee Roasters

2708 N. Green Valley Parkway, Henderson
(702) 456-1869

Single-origin cold-brewed coffee on tap is complemented by pastries made using whole wheat flour all the way from Washington state.

Rosallie Le French Café (Essential 52: see page 112)

An authentic slice of homey Southern French baking, bringing freshly made high-quality pastries and desserts to the desert.

Rose. Rabbit. Lie. (Cosmopolitan)

(702) 698-7440

Some of Ben Spungin's creations need to be seen to be believed. Chocolate dirt, anyone?

Sweets Raku (Essential 52: see page 108)

Twist (Essential 52: see page 120)

Vivian Chang creates an array of sweets that dazzle and perplex as only Gagnaire can.

Yardbird Southern Table & Bar (Venetian)

(702) 297-6541

Lots of Southern-style fried, baked, and whipped goodness.

DESSERT SAMPLER AT YARDBIRD SOUTHERN TABLE & BAR

Allegro (Essential 52: see page 26)

Located in the often overly opulent Wynn, this is an approachable place for ravioli with dandelion greens and pancetta. Reasonably priced for the venue.

TOMATO FIG MOZ SALAD AT B&B RISTORANTE

B&B Ristorante (Essential 52: see page 34)

Do visit for squid ink pasta with 'Njuda sausage or rabbit "porchetta" with Brussels sprouts from Mario Batali and Joe Bastianich.

Carbone (Essential 52: see page 42)

Waiters in velvet jackets. Veal marsala the size of a hubcap. Settle in! Bring money.

Casa di Amore

2850 E. Tropicana Avenue
(702) 433-4967

Old Vegas east of the Strip. Chow on cioppino and osso buco while being entertained by live Rat Pack-style singers. Plus, free shuttles from the Strip. Dino and Sammy would approve.

Cucina by Wolfgang Puck (The Shops at Crystals)

(702) 238-1000

The Wolf's fancy pies include tomatoey margherita and several cured wood-fired meat-laden combos.

Ferraro's Italian Restaurant & Wine Bar (Essential 52: see page 66)

Gino Ferraro has one of the best Italian wine lists in the city, and runs that rarest of creatures: a venerable Italian restaurant that's gotten better.

Fiamma Trattoria & Bar (MGM Grand)

(702) 891-7600

Pawan Pinisetti produces passels of pulchritudinous pasta, albeit in a restaurant the size of an airplane hangar.

FIAMMA TRATTORIA & BAR DINING ROOM CAFÉ AREA IN MGM GRAND

Giada (The Cromwell)

(855) 442-3271

A bit controversial for its idiosyncratic, glammed-up, and pricey interpretations of pastas and such, but this is a star-powered notable draw nonetheless.

ITALIAN LASAGNA AT NORA'S ITALIAN CUISINE

Nora's Italian Cuisine

5780 W. Flamingo Road
(702) 873-8990

A big menu packed with every conceivable variation on pastas, pizzas, and parmigianas. Recently built its own new building with a sparkling bar, patio dining, and a bocce ball court.

Pasta Shop Ristorante & Art Gallery

2525 W. Horizon Ridge Parkway, Henderson
(702) 451-1893

A funky little nook in the southern 'burbs. The house specialty of squid-ink pasta with tiger shrimp and saffron cream sauce is a must do.

Rao's (Caesars Palace)

(702) 731-7267

Sit down for serious dining with Uncle Vincent's lemon chicken, spicy meatballs, and eggplant Parmesan. After dinner, play bocce ball in the heart of the Caesars Palace pool complex.

Salute Trattoria Italiana (Red Rock Resort)

(702) 797-7311

Out in Summerlin, Salute is raising the bar for Italian food with a beautiful room and menu stars like crispy zucchini blossoms, salt-crusted baked branzino, and linguine with vodka sauce flambéed in a hollowed-out wheel of Parmesan cheese.

Sinatra (Encore)

(702) 770-5320

An elegant tribute to the Chairman of the Board offering up several of Ol' Blue Eyes' favorite dishes.

Italian (Pizza)

Amore Taste of Chicago

3945 S. Durango Drive #A8
(702) 562-9000

They make an excellent crusty deep-dish tomato pie. It's so good, even someone who doesn't love Chicago pizza will like it.

THIN CRUST, PAN, AND STUFFED PIZZAS AT AMORE TASTE OF CHICAGO

Brooksy's Bar and Grill

9295 W. Flamingo Road
(702) 562-2050

Best veggie pies in town. Eat 'em while watching live hockey in the attached ice rink.

Dom DeMarco's Pizzeria & Bar

9785 W. Charleston Boulevard
(702) 570-7000

DI FARA AT DOM DEMARCO'S PIZZERIA & BAR

Nestled in tony Summerlin, Dom's uses the recipes from Brooklyn's famous DiFara Pizza and the pies are amazing (so is the happy hour). President Obama ordered dozens of pizzas delivered during an overnight Vegas stay.

Due Forni Pizza & Wine

3555 S. Town Center Drive
(702) 586-6500

Creative wood-fired pizzas, a full menu of Italian dishes, and a big wine list way out on the west side of the valley.

Grimaldi's (several locations)

Palazzo Hotel-Casino
(702) 754-3448

Coal-fired brick ovens—just like the Brooklyn original.

Evel Pie

508 E. Fremont
(702) 840-6460

The best New York slice in Sin City is on East Fremont Street.

Metro Pizza (multiple locations)

4001 S. Decatur Boulevard
(702) 362-7896

The granddaddy of Vegas pizza joints still turns out killer pies.

Naked City Pizza Shop (multiple locations)

3240 S. Arville Street
(702) 243-6277

Buffalo-style square sheets of deep dish, beef on weck, and suicide wings.

Pizza Rock (2 locations)

Downtown Grand / Green Valley Ranch
(702) 385-0838 / (702) 616-2996

A dozen different categories of pizza, including Napoletana, Romana, Sicilian, Classic Italian, New York, New Haven, and Chicago. If you can't find something you like here, you should stop eating pizza.

3-IN-1 PIZZA AT PIZZA ROCK

Secret Pizza (Comospolitan)

(702) 698-7860

New York thin-and-crispy slices and pies available in a hidden nook (follow the vintage record-album covers down the long hallway) on the second floor of Cosmo.

Settebello Pizzeria Napoletana (2 locations)

9350 W. Sahara Avenue #170
140 S. Green Valley Parkway, Henderson
(702) 901-4877 / (702) 222-3556

This is the king of pizzerias, thanks to old-world Neapolitan standards, top-quality ingredients, and the blistering hot wood-burning ovens.

GREEN CORN TAMALES AT BORDER GRILL

MEXICAN

Border Grill (Mandalay Bay)

(702) 632-7403

The best Mexican restaurant in town to be found in a casino. The weekend brunch is a banger.

Carlito's Burritos

4300 E. Sunset Road, Henderson
(702) 547-3592

Really more New Mexican than Mexican, but the best place in town for some spicy adovada or a serious sopaipilla.

TACOS AT CHINA POBLANO

China Poblano (Cosmopolitan)

(702) 698-7900

Don't let the China-meets-Mexico vibe fool you: everything from the cochinita (Yucatan-style) barbecue pork tacos to the pozole rojo soup are some of the best versions you will ever taste.

El Menudazo

3100 E. Lake Mead Boulevard #18, North Las Vegas
(702) 944-9706

Way out of the way, up in the heart of North Las Vegas, where most gringos fear to tread. Our advice: Go for lunch and get a huge bowl of pozole.

Additional Recommendations

El Sombrero Mexican Bistro

807 S. Main Street
(702) 382-9234

Formerly the oldest operating restaurant in Sin City. It's been rehabbed and the menu redone, but it's still in its original location.

Frijoles & Frescas Grilled Tacos (multiple locations)

4811 S. Rainbow Boulevard
(702) 483-5399

Good, not great, but the frescas are fun, and the lines are out the door.

FRESH FRESCAS AT FRIJOLES & FRESCAS GRILLED TACOS

KoMex Fusion Express

633 N. Decatur Boulevard H / 4155 S. Buffalo Drive
(702) 646-1612 / (702) 778-5566

Korea-meets-Mexico-fusion-fun, or, put another way: bulgogi meets the burrito. There's nothing subtle about this food, but it's wildly and inexplicably popular with a certain sort of chowhound.

La Comida

100 S. 6th Street
(702) 463-9900

Serious Mexican cuisine and a motherlode of tequilas. A must for lovers of all things agave.

TRADITIONAL APPETIZERS AT LINDO MICHOACAN

Lindo Michoacan (multiple "Michoacan" locations)

2655 E. Desert Inn Road
(702) 735-6828

Fresh tortillas, amazing margaritas, and lots of lengua (tongue) keep us coming back to the original on East Desert Inn. The offshoots around town aren't nearly as good.

Los Antojos

2520 S. Eastern Avenue #2
(702) 457-3505

Holy hole-in-the-wall, Batman! This is the only reason ever to venture to East Sahara!

Los Molcajetes

1553 N. Eastern Avenue
(702) 633-7595

Another out of the way place on the Las Vegas/North Las Vegas border, with large volcanic molcajetes (thick, round, stone mortars) holding all sorts of spicy stews. Don't speak English? No problem, since few others in the joint do either. The servers, however, are very sweet and helpful to us gueros.

Mexican (Tacos)

Abuela's Tacos
4225 E. Sahara Avenue
(702) 431-0284

The house-made tortillas alone are worth the trip.

Los Tacos (2 locations)
1710 E. Charleston Boulevard / 4001 W. Sahara Avenue
(702) 471-7447 / (702) 252-0100

Tacos El Compita
6118 W. Charleston Boulevard
(702) 878-0008

Better than most, not as good as others.

CARNE ASADA PLATTER AT TACOS EL COMPITA

Tacos El Gordo (2 locations)
3049 S. Las Vegas Boulevard / 1724 E. Charleston Boulevard
(702) 982-5420 / (702) 251-8226

An authentic taqueria with the language barrier to prove it. Get in line and point and prepare to be impressed.

Tacos El Rodeo Barbacoa Estilo Hildago

2115 N. Decatur Boulevard
(702) 638-1100

You order at the counter and sit in a no-frills windowless room. You notice three incendiary salsas at a counter, grab a flimsy fork, and wait. Then the tacos show up and you wonder why you don't eat here every day.

QUESADILLAS AT TACOS MEXICO

Tacos Mexico (multiple locations)

1800 S. Las Vegas Boulevard
(702) 444-2288

For when you really really need a taco at 2 a.m.

Taqueria El Buen Pastor (multiple locations)

301 S. Decatur Boulevard
(702) 432-5515

Guadalajara street tacos to beat the band. Look for the taco wagon at the corner of Bonanza and Las Vegas Boulevard to nab some righteous al pastor beauties, 24/7.

SOMETHING WRONG #7 ROLL AT SUSHI FEVER

SUSHI

Hiroyoshi (Essential 52: see page 68)

Kabuto (Essential 52: see page 80)

Katsuya by Starck (SLS Las Vegas)
(702) 761-7611

I don't know what's prettier: the room, the fish, or the women who dine here.

Naked Fish's Sushi & Grill
3945 S. Durango Drive A6
(702) 228-8856

Westside hang where you're apt to see a television poker pro or two around World Series of Poker time. Check the blackboard for the live shrimp (when it's in season).

Soho Japanese Restaurant
7377 S. Jones Boulevard
(702) 776-7778

Westside sleeper, building a big reputation with sushi aficionados.

OCEAN TROUT SASHIMI AT SOHO JAPANESE RESTAURANT

Sushi Fever

7985 W. Sahara Avenue #105
(702) 838-2927

For the California-roll lover in you.

Yellowtail Japanese Restaurant & Lounge (Bellagio)

(702) 730-3900

Inventive fish. Fabulous sake list.

SEARED TUNA AT YONAKA MODERN JAPANESE

Yonaka Modern Japanese

4983 W. Flamingo Road
(702) 685-8358

The first place I send people when they ask me for an interesting restaurant off the Strip. The small-plate and raw-fish concoctions they dream up here are divine and the décor is a nice respite from the hubbub of the hotels.

Yui Edomae Sushi (Essential 52: see page 126)

Yuzu Kaiseki (see page 128)

Gorgeous, authentic omakase and kaiseki meals served to a neighborhood that has no idea how great the food is.

All-You-Can-Eat Sushi

Given all the great sushi restaurants in Vegas, the AYCE route doesn't make much sense to me. But I've included these (kicking and screaming) as the best of the bunch for those who's thing it is. (All are $21-$22 for lunch and $26-$27 for dinner.)

Blue Fin Sushi & Roll

3980 E. Sunset Road #102
(725) 696-7428

Small but mighty. One of the best neighborhood AYCE sushi joints.

Jjanga Japanese Restaurant

3650 S. Decatur Boulevard
(702) 453-3377

Not for purists—despite the name, it's Korean-run—but the product is good and this is a fun party place (or at least it can be—Jjanga had to reapply for a liquor-license, call ahead).

Oyshi Sushi (2 locations)

7775 S. Rainbow Boulevard / 7293 W. Sahara Avenue
(702) 646-9744 / (702) 485-5010

The only AYCE sushi in town that I can truly tolerate. Fresher than most. More inventive than most. More authentic than most.

Sushi House Goyemon

5255 S. Decatur Boulevard #118
(702) 331-0333

We know Japanese natives who will eat AYCE sushi only here.

FOIE GRAS NIGIRI AT SUSHI HOUSE GOYEMON

Sushi Mon (2 locations)

9770 S. Maryland Parkway #3
8320 W. Sahara Avenue #180
(702) 617-0241 / (702) 304-0044

Same owners as Goyemon. Nuff said.

ANDIRON STEAK & SEA

CHEAP EATS/ LOCAL FAVORITES

Alder & Birch (The Orleans Hotel & Casino)

(702) 365-7111

This shiny steak-centric eatery in a popular off-Strip casino features handsome modern design reminiscent of something in Seattle or San Francisco. Dine on Wagyu beef or Jidori chicken here quite more affordably than two miles east on Las Vegas Boulevard.

Andiron Steak & Sea

1720 Festival Plaza Drive
(702) 685-8002

In the summer, this place looks like a Tommy Bahama outlet. Prepare to overhear a guy in pink shorts talking about his complicated workout routine.

Big Wong (see page 141)

It's located in a strip mall with some of our priciest eateries, but everything here—noodle soups, curries, shrimp wontons—is priced below $10. The jalapeño chicken wings are insane!

Casa Don Juan (2 locations)

1204 S. Main Street / 1780 N. Buffalo Drive
(702) 384-8070 / (702) 483-5609

Getting a seat in this place is nearly impossible on weekends. Nonetheless, it's a rite of passage for southern Nevadans.

Doña Maria Tamales Restaurant

910 S. Las Vegas Boulevard
(702) 382-6538

A pilgrimage place for Las Vegans of all stripes for corn-husked masa packets.

Fat Choy Restaurant (see page 174)

A casino diner that serves the unexpected—e.g., steamed bao and duck fried rice alongside short-rib grilled cheese and kalbi steak & eggs. Expect to be impressed.

SHORT RIB GRILLED CHEESE AT FAT CHOY RESTAURANT

Fat Greek Mediterranean Bistro

4001 S. Decatur Boulevard #34
(702) 222-0666

Family-owned hot spot for lunch, TFG serves authentic Greek/Armenian fare made from scratch. Leave room for the awesome desserts and pastries.

Flock & Fowl

380 W. Sahara Avenue
(626) 616-6632

Poached chicken, shmaltz rice, broth, and dips. So simple, but there's a reason why it's one of the most popular dishes in Asia. Good chicken wings and bombastic bao.

Forte European Tapas Bar & Bistro

4180 S. Rainbow Boulevard
(702) 220-3876

This Bulgarian-Armenian-Hungarian-Greek-Russian-Spanish tapas bar has been a hit with foodies and Vegas' Central European community since day one. Don't miss the flavored vodkas or a chat with owner Nina Manchev.

Harrie's Bagelmania

855 E. Twain Avenue #120
(702) 369-3322

Bagels, smoked fish, bountiful breakfasts, and big deli sandwiches till closing at 3 p.m.

Home Plate Grill & Bar

2460 W. Warm Springs Road
(702) 410-5600

A sports bar that takes its food seriously. Serves up excellent pizzas and one of the best clam chowders in town.

Honey Salt

1031 S. Rampart Boulevard
(702) 445-6100

Soccer-mom food.

John Mull's Meats & Road Kill Grill (2 locations)

3730 Thom Boulevard / 11357 N. Decatur Boulevard
(702) 645-1200 / (702) 863-1528

This butcher shop, on a ranch in a residential area way up on the north side of town, serves combo plates of barbecued ribs, brisket, hot links, rib tips, pork tri-tip, and chicken, with apple or peach cobbler for dessert.

CHICKEN PLATE AT JOHN MULL'S MEATS & ROAD KILL GRILL

Kitchen Table

1716 W. Horizon Ridge Parkway #100
(702) 478-4782

Somewhat remotely located near the edge of Henderson, this modernistic kitchen serves upscale breakfasts and lunches daily inside or on the patio.

GRILLED OYSTERS AT LOLA'S—A LOUISIANA KITCHEN

Lola's—A Louisiana Kitchen (2 locations)

241 W. Charleston Boulevard / 1220 N. Town Center Drive
(702) 227-5652 / (702) 871-5652

Good gumbo, jambalaya, étouffée, po boys, and killer charbroiled oysters.

Lulu's Bread & Breakfast (see page 178)

In other cities across the western U.S., eateries like Lulu's are the norm. In Las Vegas, it stands out for all the morning and midday reasons. The perfect stop on the way to hiking at Mt. Charleston.

Mary's Hash House

2605 S. Decatur Boulevard #103
(702) 873-9479

Not "a go go"! Corned beef, roast beef, ham, chicken, or combo hash, served with grits and homemade jellies.

M&M Soul Food Café (2 locations)

3923 W. Charleston Boulevard / 2211 S. Las Vegas Boulevard
(702) 453-7685 / (702) 478-5767

This nondescript lunch counter puts forth superb fried chicken and waffles, cornbread, collard greens, corned-beef hash, and decent-enough barbecued ribs to almost make you think you're in Mississippi.

Nora's Italian Cuisine (see page 182)

This long-operating local fave serves large portions off a big menu with almost nothing priced at more than $20. In a new (and bigger) location, it's now an after-work hotspot.

MELROSE PASTA AT NORA'S ITALIAN CUISINE

Norm's Diner

3945 S. Durango Drive #A1
(702) 431-3447

Possibly the largest breakfast menu in town, from omelets and Benedicts to pancakes and frittatas—even an off-menu creamed chipped beef on toast. Breakfast and lunch only.

Other Mama (Essential 52: see page 102)

Paymon's Mediterranean Café & Lounge (2 locations)

4147 S. Maryland Parkway / 8380 W. Sahara Avenue
(702) 731-6030 / (702) 804-0293

Barely average Mediterranean fare, but the extended-happy hour prices have made these a favorite among the undiscerning.

Perú Chicken Rotisserie (2 locations)

2055 E. Tropicana / 3886 W. Sahara Avenue
(702) 732-0079 / (702) 982-0073

The rotisserie chicken is good, but the prize here is the ceviche, made with chunks of "premier" sea bass and served with potato, corn, and toasted corn on the side.

Roma Deli & Restaurant (2 locations)

5755 W. Spring Mountain Road / 8524 W. Sahara Avenue
(702) 871-5577 / (702) 228-2264

This bustling Italian restaurant, deli, and bakery is the real deal for lunch or dinner. Try a hot or cold sub on their fresh-baked bread. Warning: The cookies are addictive.

ITALIAN SUB AT ROMA DELI & RESTAURANT

Sin City Smokers Barbecue & Catering

2861 N. Green Valley Parkway, Henderson
(702) 823-5605

SIN CITY SMOKERS BARBECUE & CATERING

Las Vegas is where barbecue goes to die. Whenever good 'cue has come to these parts, it hasn't lasted. The shitty stuff hangs around forever. SCS just may buck that trend, with smoked meats and sides that are seriously succulent.

Tap House

5589 W. Charleston Boulevard
(702) 870-2111

Famed for its pizza and wings (half-price late nights and all weekend). Monday's free open-mic sessions pack the back room with aging mobsters and their dolled-up dames—real-life time traveling!

The Blind Pig

4515 Dean Martin Drive
(702) 430-4444

Though in a rather hard-to-find yet "it's right there!" location in the Panorama Towers west of the Strip, this comfortable brick-lined restaurant melds diner-style grub with good Italian dinner service.

Todd's Unique Dining

4350 E. Sunset Road, Henderson
(702) 259-8633

Todd Clore is at the stoves every night, keeping Henderson well-fed and giving us a reason to travel there.

Vila Algarve

6120 W. Tropicana Avenue #11-12
(702) 666-3877

Family-owned and serving authentic Portuguese cuisine, with a splash of Greek and a penchant for seafood.

Vintner Grill

10100 W. Charleston Boulevard #150
(702) 214-5590

Nothing about this place is as good as its reputation.

Zaytoon Market & Restaurant

3655 S. Durango Drive #11-14
(702) 685-1875

Located on the west side, Zaytoon is an in-the-know place for Persian cuisine. The hummus is among the best in town.

BEEF KOOBIDEH AND CHICKEN KABOB AT ZAYTOON MARKET & RESTAURANT

Bootlegger Italian Bistro
7700 S. Las Vegas Boulevard
(702) 736-4939

Former Strip singer and lieutenant governor Lorraine Hunt's family has owned the Bootlegger since 1949. It's changed locations over the years, but it still relies on the same tried-and-true family recipes. And you never know what Strip performers might stop by late at night to work out some new material on the dining-room stage.

SONNY CHARLES AT BOOTLEGGER ITALIAN BISTRO

Chicago Joe's Restaurant
820 S. 4th Street
(702) 382-5637

It's a downtown institution, but old-time fare like minestrone soup and spaghetti and meatballs is about the best you can hope for here.

FRANK SINATRA'S BOOTH AT GOLDEN STEER STEAKHOUSE

Golden Steer Steakhouse
308 W. Sahara Avenue
(702) 384-4470

With a tuxedoed maître d', oversized booths dedicated to the celebrities that once frequented them, and cowboy art and memorabilia on the walls, a meal at the Golden Steer is a walk back through its 50-something-year history. The Rat Packers all ate here and plaques over selected tables designate where they sat.

Hitchin' Post Saloon and Steakhouse

3650 N. Las Vegas Boulevard
(702) 644-1220

A classic value-steakhouse located on the far north end of Las Vegas Boulevard with complete steak dinners priced under $20. Eat in the little enclosed steak room, at the bar, or on the outside patio next to a horseshoe pit.

Hugo's Cellar (Four Queens)

(702) 385-4011

Ladies are presented with a rose as they enter this fine-dining restaurant in the basement of the Four Queens, and after your meal you get a selection of chocolate-dipped figs, apricots, and strawberries. In between, there's attentive tableside service and butter handcrafted into the shape of a rose. Just like in 1978.

Italian-American Club Restaurant

2333 E. Sahara Avenue
(702) 457-3866

Operating since 1961, the IAC was originally a men's social club boasting a membership that included Frank Sinatra, along with several other showbiz and "sporting" types. Those kinds of guys still come around, but it's mostly for the pasta and live entertainment.

Lawry's The Prime Rib

4043 Howard Hughes Parkway
(702) 893-2223

Though born in L.A. and not a true Vegas original, it's been here long enough to be vibrantly vintage. It does perfect prime rib and Yorkshire pudding in a clubby timeless setting.

HERO SPINACH AT LAWRY'S THE PRIME RIB

Michael's Gourmet Room (South Point)

(702) 796-7111

It's totally overpriced, so try to get a casino comp. Try the veal Française and the Caesar salad, mixed tableside, then try to stiffle a yawn.

Mt. Charleston Lodge

5375 Kyle Canyon Road
(702) 872-5408

Escape the heat by driving up to Mt. Charleston Lodge for the elk, buffalo, and traditional burgers. Bring your pooch and eat on the doggie deck.

SPINACH AND MUSHROOM OMELET AT OMELET HOUSE

Omelet House (multiple locations)

2160 W. Charleston
(702) 384-6868

A long-time locals fave, a booth is reserved for famous former Mayor Oscar Goodman and his wife Carolyn, the current mayor.

Pamplemousse Le Restaurant

400 E. Sahara Avenue
(702) 733-2066

A Gallic joint named by crooner Bobby Darin that somehow hasn't given up the ghost.

Peppermill Restaurant and Fireside Lounge

2985 S. Las Vegas Boulevard
(702) 735-7635

Visiting the Peppermill at night, basking in its neon glow and getting buzzed, is a de rigueur locals rite of passage.

SCORPION DRINKS AT PEPPERMILL RESTAURANT AND FIRESIDE LOUNGE

Piero's Italian Cuisine

355 Convention Center Drive
(702) 369-2305

A certain type of middle-manager/car salesman/real-estate huckster-type will tell you Piero's is the greatest Italian restaurant in town. They tend to be the parents of the lounge lizards who think the same thing about Panevino.

Pioneer Saloon

310 NV-161, Goodsprings
(702) 874-9362

A 45-minute drive southwest of Vegas brings you to the unmistakable Pioneer Saloon in the wilds of the Mojave Desert. It's great, especially when there's live music. Try the Ghost BBQ Burger (fired with the magma-like Bhut jolokia pepper) and a cold beevo, or get caveman fancy with a huge tomahawk ribeye steak for two. It's been here since 1913. Bikers and photographers love this place.

The Bagel Café

301 N. Buffalo Drive
(702) 255-3444

Nevada movers and shakers, plus many others, flock here for big breakfasts, bialys, and a worthy matzoh-ball soup.

Top of Binion's Steakhouse (Binion's Gambling Hall)

(702) 382-1600

Venture to the 24th floor of the namesake downtown casino to enjoy chicken-fried lobster and a glass of vino with one of the best views in town.

Vickie's Diner

1700 S. Las Vegas Boulevard
(702) 444-4459

Known for decades as White Cross Drugs, this diner, located between the north end of the Strip and downtown, is still serving breakfasts, burgers, and more, 24/7.

GHOST BURGER AT PIONEER SALOON

THE BOBBIE AT CAPRIOTTI'S

LATE NIGHT

The best place to research hundreds of late-night Vegas restaurants is LasVegasAdvisor.com; in the top navigation menu, hover over Eat, then click on Restaurants. On the Restaurants landing page, click on Advanced Restaurant Search, then select the Late Night box near the top. Note that almost all the casino coffee shops and many of the noodle bars are open with 24 hours or into the wee hours. Here are some of the most popular, convenient, and best late-night eateries.

American Coney Island (the D)

(702) 388-2120

For exactly 100 years, these Dearborn Sausage-brand hot dogs, topped with fine mustard, sweet chopped onions, and a secret family-recipe chili sauce, have been a favorite of Detroiters. The location at the D is this stand's first location outside Michigan. Open 24 hours daily.

Bootlegger Italian Bistro (see page 205)

Open 24 hours daily.

Capriotti's Sandwich Shop (multiple locations)

4480 Paradise Road
(702) 736-6166

The one Capriotti's that's open day and night is convenient to the partyers at the Hard Rock.

Casa di Amore (see page 180)

Open Wed.-Mon. until 5 a.m.

Chada Street/Chada Thai (Essential 52: see page 48)

Open Sun.-Tues. until 3 a.m.

Food Express (Palace Station)

(702) 367-2411

Surprisingly authentic Chinese food in this venerable off-Strip casino (with plenty of free parking); it's known for lobster, abalone, duck feet, and jellyfish. Open daily until 3 a.m.

Hash House A Go-Go (LINQ)

(702) 254-4646

Monster portions of oversized pancakes, breakfast scrambles, hashes, Benedicts, and other breakfasts have given this chain an almost cult following; they also serve a casual lunch and dinner. Open daily 24 hours.

Hexx Kitchen + Bar (see page 178)

Centrally located with a recommendable menu, Hexx is open 24 hours a day. The patio generally closes at midnight, but that that can vary, depending on the weather. If it's open and warm out, it's a fine people-watching opportunity.

PATIO AT HEXX KITCHEN + BAR

Honey Pig (see page 149)

Open daily 24 hours.

Hong Kong Garden Seafood & BBQ Café

3407 S. Jones Boulevard
(702) 878-8838

Late-night hot pot. Open daily until 6 a.m.

THAI YELLOW CURRY WITH SHRIMP AND JASMINE STEAMED RICE AT KRUNG SIAM THAI

Krung Siam Thai (see page 152)

Open daily until 5:30 a.m.

Musashi Japanese Steakhouse

3900 Paradise Road
(702) 735-4744

Sushi, teppanyaki, and a late-night happy hour are the big draws here. Open daily until 4 a.m.

Peppermill Restaurant (see page 208)

Coffee-shop fare in a veteran of decades on the Strip. Open daily 24 hours.

Ping Pang Pong (see page 144)

Open daily until 3 a.m.

Pin-Up Pizza (Planet Hollywood)

(702) 785-5888

Each New York thin-crust slice is the size of 2-1/2 regular slices at less than twice the price. Open daily until 4 a.m.

Raku (Essential 52: see page 108)

This place typically bustles right up until the final seating. Open daily until 2 a.m.

Secret Pizza (see page 185)

Open daily until 5 a.m.

Vickie's Diner (see page 209)

This is the oldest diner in Las Vegas, at the same location as when it was Tiffany's, the counter at the defunct White Cross Drugs. A classic, serving three meals, all available 24/7/365.

White Castle (see page 176)

In case of a center Strip emergency where you must have food! now!, you can get some fast-food (and nostalgic) sliders at the 24/7 White Castle next to Casino Royale.

Wolfgang Puck Bar & Grill (MGM Grand)

(702) 891-3000

This shrine to classic California cuisine opens wide onto the casino floor, so it's lively and busy, even as the sun is coming up. Open daily until 6 a.m.

GRILLED POTATO CHIPS AT WOLFGANG PUCK BAR & GRILL

THE CHAIN GANG

Every major and most minor restaurant chain is represented in Las Vegas. Here are the ones that, for whatever reason, are the most popular, frequented, or critically acclaimed.

Capriotti's (see page 211)

Founded in Wilmington, Delaware, in 1976, Capriotti's is now based in Las Vegas and has more than 100 company-owned and franchised sandwich shops in 17 states. It's known for cold, grilled, and veggie subs made from home-roasted turkey, hand-pulled meats, and a special cole slaw. The Bobbie (pulled turkey, cranberry sauce, and stuffing) is the signature sandwich.

Chick-fil-A (multiple locations)

One of the last major chains to locate to Nevada and the 46th state for this chain to locate in, Atlanta-based all-chicken Chick-fil-A (the "fil-a" part of the name is believed to be a play on "fillet") opened its first two Vegas locations in 2016. A third opened in 2017,with plans to open 8-10 total locations in Nevada through 2021.

Cracker Barrel

8350 Dean Martin Drive / 2815 E. Craig Road
(702) 474-1120 / (702) 457-1200

Like Chick-fil-A, Cracker Barrel opened its first store in Nevada and 639th in 43 states in 2016 and locals immediately went nuts for the chicken and dumplings, meat loaf, fried chicken, steaks, catfish, and wholesome fixin's. Visitors without cars can take the free Silverton shuttle to the one next door to the far south casino.

Dave & Busters

2130 Park Center Drive #100, Downtown Summerlin
(702) 984-4800

A third chain that opened here in 2016, this was Dallas-based Dave & Buster's 87th location. It's a combination sports bar and arcade, with more than 200 video, laser, and tables for adult gamers, located way out on the western edge of the valley and catering, as such, almost entirely to locals.

Giordano's (Grand Bazaar Shops, Bally's)

(702) 850-2420

Launched in 1974 in Chicago, this deep dish is the reason that pizza is called a "pie"—the crust encloses a sort of casserole. Giordano's has won every Chicago pizza award and you can stretch the mootz from there to the center Las Vegas Strip.

LUNCH SPECIAL AT GIORDANO'S

In-N-Out Burger (see page 175)

This insanely popular and family-owned chain invaded Vegas in 1992 (the first location is at the corner of Tropicana and Dean Martin Drive) and now has 15 locations around the valley. Be prepared to wait in a long line if you're at any one of them during prime lunch or dinner times.

Shake Shack (see page 175)

Starting out as a literal shack in Manhattan in 2004, Shake Shack offerings don't, in our estimation, quite justify this chain's explosive growth. A sort of high-tech high-priced In-N-Out Burger, the visitor version is at New York-New York.

PEOPLE/ CELEBRITY WATCHING

MEHCAD BROOKS AT ANDIAMO STEAKHOUSE

Andiamo Steakhouse (the D)

(702) 388-2460

The D's Italian Steakhouse has proven to be a hit with the famous friends of flamboyant casino owner Derek Stevens, including stars of UFC, WWE, and NASCAR and the casts of TV's "Pawn Stars" and "Sons of Anarchy."

Bazaar Meat (Essential 52: see page 32)

"This is why you are here!" chef José Andrés—who eats whatever makes him "feel like a lion"—roars from the menu, but there are no human sacrifices of starlets or socialites in the fire pit and this restaurant's vibe is designed to be as playful as the cuisine and its creator.

Border Grill (see page 187)

Patio views of the famous Lazy River at Mandalay Beach, or of the hordes enjoying some high-end retail therapy in the Forum Shops—take your pick from the "Too Hot Tamales" two Vegas locations, both of which offer plenty of people-watching potential from a relaxed, social vantage point.

CRUSH (MGM Grand)

(702) 891-3222

If you want to catch Rick Moonen nibbling on gnocchi, George Strait savoring a steak, Dita Von Teese dining on a Date & Artichoke Flatbread, or Bruce Buffer toying with Tuna 2 Ways, this place would be your best bet to do it.

CUT (Essential 52: see page 54)

Proprietor Wolfgang Puck knows the whole of Hollywood and many of his famous fans choose to get their steak fix here when slumming in Vegas.

Hexx Kitchen + Bar (see page 178)

The new hangout for sweet-toothed celebs—from rapper 50 Cent to Playmate Kennedy Summers—is also giving neighbor Mon Ami Gabi a run for its money, with its matching patio views of the passing hoi polloi on Las Vegas Boulevard.

La CAVE (Essential 52: see page 86)

Katy Perry, Amber Rose, Troy Aikman, Neil Patrick Harris, Yeardley Smith, Michael McDonald, Patrick Monahan, Sebastian Maniscalco, Kenny Mayne, Nick Cannon, Akon—it would probably be quicker to list the celebrities who haven't yet been spotted at this place.

LAVO Italian Restaurant (Palazzo)

(702) 791-1800

This perennially popular "haute" spot has added an extra dimension to its restaurant/nightclub offerings, with the debut of LAVO Casino Club, where grand-opening night saw rapper Busta Rhymes joining celebrity host, actor Joe Manganiello, at the blackjack tables.

JOE MANGANIELLO AT LAVO ITALIAN RESTAURANT

Mon Ami Gabi (see page 166)

With perfect views of the Bellagio Fountains, this French bistro overlooking the Strip remains among our top picks for observing the herd on the street.

MR CHOW (Essential 52: see page 100)

The seventh wonder from Michael Chow is where J. Lo chose to celebrate her opening night at Planet Hollywood, and is also where (show)room-mate Britney Spears' held her big New Year's Day bash.

Old Homestead Steakhouse (Caesars Palace)

(702) 731-7560

From DJ megastar Calvin Harris, to actor Morgan Freeman, you never know who might be dining at this Las Vegas transplant of the historic New York original that claims to be the inventor of the doggy bag.

Rx Boiler Room (Mandalay Place)

(702) 632-7200

Celebrity chef (Rick Moonen) has lots of celebrity friends who tend to pop into his celebrity-friendly "steampunk" bistro as a prelude to a night of partying at MBay.

RICK MOONEN AT RX BOILER ROOM

Sonny's Saloon

3449 Sammy Davis Jr Drive
(702) 731-5553

Sonny's claimed its place in infamy as the ransom-drop-off location in the 1993 kidnapping of Steve Wynn's daughter. Known back then as a hangout for off-shift casino employees, not much changed; the customers start pouring in around 11 p.m., with a mix of old-timers, dealers, dancers, and other working types who make for some amazing only-in-Vegas people watching.

GAVIN ROSEDALE FROM BUSH AT STK IN THE COSMOPOLITAN

STK Las Vegas (Cosmopolitan)

(702) 698-7990

From Tony Romo and Andre Agassi, to Halle Berry and Jessica Alba, via Robin Thicke and Dan Aykroyd, the steakhouse at Cosmo can certainly boast some star-studded carnivores among its clientele.

TAO Asian Bistro (Venetian/Grand Canal Shoppes)

(702) 388-8338

If gossip maven Perez Hilton chooses to dine here when he's in town, you know his likely won't be the only famous face in the house.

SPECIAL DIET

CRUSH (see page 218)

Special diets must be cool, because this celebrity hotspot at MGM Grand caters to almost all of them: vegetarian, vegan, gluten-free, dairy-free, and seafood/shellfish-free options.

EATT (see page 60)

French cuisine with a health-conscious spin.

ENDIVE AT EATT GOURMET BISTRO

Komol Restaurant

953 E. Sahara Avenue E-10
(702) 731-6542

A huge MSG-free Thai menu composed entirely of vegan and vegetarian options.

Lazeez Indian-Mediterranean Grill

8560 W. Desert Inn Road
(702) 778-1613

This Indian-Middle Eastern halal grill serves a menu that includes an array of vegan, vegetarian, and gluten-free options.

Mint Indian Bistro (2 locations)

730 E. Flamingo Road / 4246 S. Durango
(702) 894-9334 / (702) 247-4610

One of Las Vegas' top Indian restaurants, Mint caters to a variety of special-diet needs, including vegan, vegetarian, and gluten-free, separate vegan and vegetarian versions of the chef's tasting menu, and a good lunch buffet; this is also the place for organic/vegan wine.

Osi's Kitchen

4604 W. Sahara Avenue #6
(702) 826-2727

This Mediterranean-Moroccan café specializes in glatt-kosher fare, including a range of catering menus for Shabbat dinner.

VegeNation

618 Carson Avenue
(702) 366-8515

Open for breakfast through dinner, this downtown eatery is 100% plant-based and seasoned with their own herbs; there are also a dedicated kids' menu and a full bar that uses cold-pressed juices. Gluten-free dishes are marked on the menu.

Veggie House (see page 145)

Violette's Vegan Organic Café & Juice Bar

8560 W. Desert Inn Road
(702) 685-0466

Veggie-laden creations and smoothies galore. The Violette is Cyndi Violette, one of the original "poker babes" and a World Series of Poker bracelet winner (2004).

FRUIT JUICES AT VIOLETTE'S VEGAN ORGANIC CAFÉ & JUICE BAR

Wynn/Encore

Every Wynn Resorts restaurant offers a "secret" veggie-friendly menu. You will need to ask your server to see it. Also noteworthy, the Buffet at Wynn is renowned for its sugar-free dessert options.

2013 CHATEAU MUSAR JEUNE ROUGE AT CHADA THAI AND WINE

GRAPE EXPECTATIONS
(LAS VEGAS' BEST WINE DRINKING)

Las Vegas isn't really a "wine bar" sort of town. Wine bars generally require a certain level of introspection and contemplation and Las Vegas generally is about as contemplative as a UFC cage match. But this doesn't mean there aren't fabulous places to indulge your taste for fermented grapes. What it does mean is that you have to go to some of our finer restaurants to find wines (by the glass or bottle) that will blow your socks off.

Below are my 12 favorite sipping venues, places where our town's great sommeliers take enormous pride in pouring vintages from around the globe—wines you can drink, or think about, to your palate's content.

Estiatorio Milos

Greek wines may be unpronounceable, but they're delicious. They're also substantially underpriced compared to similar seafood-friendly wines from France and Italy. Don't even try to master the odd lisps and tongue rolls of Assyrtiko, Moshofilero, or Mavrodaphne.

Just point and smile, or ask the staff for help. (I promise they won't make fun of you.) Anyone who orders anything but Greek wines with this food should be sentenced to a year of drinking Harvey Wallbangers.

Restaurant Guy Savoy

The list is as thick as a dictionary and, at first blush, not for the faint of heart or parsimonious of purse. But look closely and you'll find a surprising number of bargains for less than $100. Or ask sommelier Phil Park and he'll happily point them out to you. The champagne bar is where you'll find serious oenophiles perusing the list a full half-hour before their reservation, just like they do it in France.

Chada Street/Chada Thai

These sister restaurants are a few miles apart, but connected by a love of white wines that owner Bon Atcharawan has successfully brought to Chinatown. Both lists are deep in Rieslings and chardonnays; the champagne selection at Chada Street puts most Strip lists to shame and at decidedly gentler prices. It's not for nothing that every sommelier in Las Vegas treats both of these venues like their personal after-hours clubs.

Marché Bacchus

A pinot noir wall, lakeside dining, and the gentlest mark-ups in town ($10 over retail) make MB a must-stop on any wine-lover's tour of Vegas. Jeff and Rhonda Wyatt are always there to help you choose a glass or a case of whatever mainstream cab or off-beat syrah suits your fancy. Or do what I do: Just stick with Burgundy and go nuts.

Ferraro's Italian Restaurant & Wine Bar

What I love about Italian wines is what I love about Italians and Italian food: They're friendly, passionate, fiercely regional, and confusing in a good way. Don't know your Montelcinos from your Montepulcianos? Nessun problema. Geno Ferraro is always there to help you parse the Barbarescos from the Barolos. One of the greatest Italian lists in America is at one of our finest Italian restaurants.

Bazaar Meat

I don't understand Spanish wine any more than I understand how José Andrés can have so much energy and so many great restaurants. But the next best thing to knowing a lot about a country's wines is knowing a sommelier who is eager to teach you. In Las Vegas, Chloe Helfand is that gal. She's always there with a smile and a lip-smacking wine you don't know made with a grape you've never heard of. Which is one of the reasons we love sommeliers. And Chloe.

La Cave

Mark Hefter's wine program is a lot like Mark Hefter: fun, interesting, intelligent, and all over the map. Hefter has poured wine from Le Cirque 2000 in New York to Spago and Circo in Las Vegas and needless to say, the man knows his grapes. With over 50 wines by the glass, he can dazzle anyone, from the novice drinker to the dedicated oenophile. But what we love about his list is its eclecticism.

At La Cave, you can dip your toe into the world's most interesting

wines at very friendly price points. Curious about those orange and pink wines that are all the rage these days? Here's where to start.

Carnevino

If your measure of a great wine bar is the number of wines by the glass offered, look elsewhere. If you rate your wine tasting by quality—of the breadth and depth of the list, the bar snacks, the staff, and the mixology (should you stray into creative boozy territory)—then this is your place. The list is conveniently located inside the (massive) menu and the mark-ups are not for the timid. But the excellence of everything, from the steaks and pastas to the super Tuscan verticals, will take your breath away.

Lotus of Siam

Robert Parker (yeah, that Robert Parker) calls Lotus' wine card the greatest for German wines in America and we have no reason to argue with him. It's also shoulder-deep in sake, Alsatian whites, and Austrian Grüner Veltliners—all of which match (in surprising ways) Saipan Chutima's fierce and fiery country-Thai cooking. This is where you'll find almost every wine professional in town on their day off, usually at a table groaning with bottles of Riesling.

Sage

The trouble with Sage is that the food is so good, sometimes you forget about the wine, and the wine list is so good, sometimes you forget about the food. I like California pinot noir and chardonnay with Shawn McClain's innovative fare, but the list covers the world in all areas of consequence. Such choices here are a happy conundrum to experience, whether you're dining or hanging out in the stunning bar.

Hearthstone

Great wine drinking in the 'burbs is harder to find than a corner without a fast-food franchise. Hearthstone deserves props for actually having a wine program and for a list that breaks down according to varietal character—"Big Reds," "Crisp, Clean & Lean," "Voluptuous But Light," etc. The by-the-glass selection is solid, but what really gets my attention is the half-off Monday-night specials, which allow for some serious drinking of some serious bottles.

NEW ADDITIONS AT LOTUS OF SIAM

Epilogue

So there you have it, my tour of the greatest restaurants in one of the best restaurant cities on Earth, along with the best advice I can give about how to enjoy yourself when you're dining out.

It's been quite a ride these past 23 years. I've weathered divorce, substance abuse, and failures both professional and personal. Through it all, I've had the restaurants of Las Vegas to soothe my soul and keep me company. Through thousands of meals, a smiling hostess, a solicitous waiter, and fabulous food and drink have always consoled me. For years, through many of those trying times, the only thing that kept me going (and, to be frank, kept me in Las Vegas) were the wonderful meals waiting for me a short drive from my house.

I calculate that I have gained about a pound for every year I've been writing about the Las Vegas food scene and I wear those pounds proudly. They're a testament to the great chefs who have fed me. They're my salute to some of the best cooking on Earth.

Even so, I'm still searching for my perfect meal. I might never find it, but I have a pretty good idea of what it looks like.

My Perfect Meal

Like all obsessives, I'm constantly looking for perfection in the object of my desire. It doesn't exist, of course, but dreaming about it, like any dream, is fun. Besides, after approximately 20,000 restaurant meals over 50 years, I have an opinion or two about what constitutes the ideal restaurant meal.

My perfect meal would be on a Thursday or Friday, never on a Saturday. Saturday night is for rubes, when kitchens and staffs are stressed to the max. Thursdays are when the produce and chefs are the freshest. Most protein shipments arrive around midweek (in anticipation of the big weekend), so you're getting first dibs on whatever seafood or produce fits your fancy.

My perfect meal would be at a restaurant with which I'm familiar, but not one where I've been so many times that I can recite the menu. The staff would know me and that I was there with serious intentions, but not be so friendly as to treat me like an old friend. Upon arrival (20-30 minutes ahead of my guests), I would be shown a seat at the bar or lounge, be handed a glass of vintage or grower champagne, along with the wine list, which I'd peruse with the intensity of a microbiologist wrangling a stem cell. About two-thirds of the way through my glass, it would be politely refilled after barely a nod between me and the wine waiter. In another 15 minutes, the head sommelier would appear and chat me up; he'd suggest a bottle or two to start the meal. There would then be an agreement to re-visit the subject once my party and I had taken our seats.

There would be no music, not even the suggestion thereof. If a strolling band of mariachis appeared near the front door, they would be shooed away. (Mariachi is the only food-friendly music I can stand … when I'm eating Mexican food, in a Mexican restaurant, in Mexico.) If Yo-Yo Ma walked in and offered to play a personal concert for me, at my table, he'd be 86'd so fast his cello would be spinning. If a food server was caught whistling the "Hallelujah" chorus, he'd have his mouth taped shut. The only sounds in the restaurant would be of tinkling glasses and murmured conversation. Music in restaurants ruins both the music and the food.

We'd be seated and my guests would be offered champagne. If there were four of us, we'd be in a discreet booth somewhere on the side of the restaurant. If it were the Food Gal and I, we'd sit side by side at a banquette. The linens would be thick and the napkin the size of a bedsheet. Plates would be white; stemware would be thin. Any stupid flowers or fake candles would've been whisked away before I was shown my seat. German sparkling mineral water would be the palate-scraping thirst-quenching beverage of choice.

There would be cheese to be admired as we were strolling to our seats, but there would be oysters, lots of them—preferably from northern France; otherwise from the Pacific Northwest. Accompanying these would be the last of the champagne and a bottle of crisp, mineral-rich, grand cru Chablis to sustain us through the early courses.

The question of appetizers and the ubiquitous amuse bouche is a tricky one. This is one area where Spanish molecular gastronomy

has its place. You want things to be tasty, salty, and intriguing, but you don't want to kill your appetite or your palate. Whatever foam or gelée José Andrés or Pierre Gagnaire is tossing my way would do quite nicely. There would also be ham. Italians also get it right with simple prosciutto and melon and Spain has conquered the world with its acorn-fed jamón iberico de bellota pata negra. A tender slice of one or a few chips of the other would be de rigueur. Magically, a small glass of oloroso sherry would appear with the ham—my waiter knowing that this is the only thing to drink with ham.

Sometime around the end of these early courses, the wine steward would reappear and discuss what we planned for our main dishes. Having spoken to me earlier, he'd know something of my preferences and either confirm my selection or offer an alternative by stating, "If you like the Bonnes Mares, sir, might I suggest a Grand Echezeaux?" Of course, we would then get both by way of comparison.

Service would be fast, not overly friendly, and nearly invisible. There would be no introductions beyond a stating of one's name; there would be no asking, "Is everything delicious?" or "Is everything prepared to your liking?" Water glasses would remain filled, crumbs swept away before you even knew they were there.

Bread would be offered, but not too fast. Not because I don't like bread at the start of my meal, but because I like it too much. If you've ever seen the bread carts at Guy Savoy and Joël Robuchon, you know they're heaven on Earth for a carbo-king like yours truly. Dozens of offerings—from saffron milk bread and brioche to classic baguettes—are paraded before you, all irresistible. And since we can resist anything but temptation, these odes to oven-baked bliss are a trap into which we too easily fall. One of each, please, after the appetizers, along with butter (salted and un-) from Normandy, France.

Then would come the soup. Soups have fallen into disfavor in America; they're too hard to make well and aren't flashy or sexy or instagrammable. Very few soups look like anything but a bowl of colored liquid with something floating in it. But a great soup is the distillation of the chef's art, intensifying and extracting every bit of flavor from whatever goes into it. Thus can a simple vichyssoise be as transporting as a bracing gazpacho. A great soup also revives the appetite. The soup at my perfect meal would be either vegetable- or seafood-based, cold in the summer and hot in the winter. Secretly, it would be my measure of the chef's talent.

Wine, of course, would accompany the soup. Riesling most definitely, either from the Mosel or Alsace. (Two different styles, I know; I'll drink anything I want in my own fantasy.) No meal is worth its salt if there aren't at least five empty wine bottles on the table at its end.

For the intermezzo: an entire lobe of foie gras (like the one at Michael Mina) served with a huckleberry compote, buttered brioche, and a late-harvest (vendange tardive) gewurtztraminer so unctuous it could coat the back of a spoon, with a finish that lasted until next Thursday.

Then, in languorous order, there would be a starch (white-truffle risotto would do nicely), followed by a seafood (Dungeness crab, Copper River king salmon, langoustines the size of small lobsters, Dover sole, wild North Atlantic turbot). The fish would be on the bone, simple in its presentation. Before we got to the beef, we would want to stretch the chefs, and all simplicity would be dispensed with. And there's no better way to deliciously complicate things than with little birds. Especially little birds encased in pastry. Something like cailles en sarcophage (quails in a sarcophagus of puff pastry) smothered in truffles, would do quite nicely, thank you. Then the beef, either six-month dry-aged Black Angus, or Charolais, or one of those old Spanish cows ringed with yellow-orange fat the color of an autumn sunset, and it would be served with a quart of tarragon-rich Béarnaise. Grand cru Burgundies would accompany the beef and premier cru Burgundies would wash down the fish. (The greatest white chardonnays can obscure the delicacy of fine fish, just as most California wines obliterate the taste of almost anything in their path.) There would be English peas and German asparagus in season, and Robuchon potatoes no matter what month it was. My wife would get the rack of lamb, not because she loves Colorado lamb, but because I'd want to see how it tastes with the '97 Ducru-Beaucaillou or '90 Cheval Blanc we just uncorked.

Cheese has been described as milk's leap into immortality and the cheeses on my table would be a picture of divinity—English Stilton, Roquefort, Parmigiano-Reggiano, crumbly Castelmagno, creamy Camembert, stinky Munster—presented with Comice and Anjou pears at their peak of ripeness and a vintage port so old, the label would be in hieroglyphics.

Dessert would be a simple affair—a table groaning under a blizzard of selections from chocolate-chip cookies to a Grand Marnier soufflé straight from the oven, including whatever magic the pastry chef might be weaving with seasonal fruits lying around. Crème

brûlée would be among them, along with a construct of mille-feuille pastry so light, it would shatter when struck by merely a glance.

Finally, dessert wine. Dessert wines are problematical, not because they aren't good, but because they're too good. The great ones stand alone as desserts unto themselves and should be appreciated as such (although they also go spectacularly well with cheese). My greatest repast would end with at least three of them: a Sauternes, a trockenbeerenauslese, and a Madeira so ancient that Methuselah's mother probably served them at his bar mitzvah.

The postscript to a meal like this would have to include a digestivo or two from one of those post-prandial carts Mario Batali has wheeling around his restaurants. No coffee. Offering coffee (and all that acid) after such a meal only compounds whatever stress your gastrointestinals are under. Coffee is a daytime drink. Americans have yet to figure this out. Just as they have yet to discover that the only sound you need at a great meal is the conversation among friends and loved ones appreciating one another, and the wonderful food everyone is being served.

SPARROW + WOLF

Section III

Index and Maps

Essential 52 Restaurants Index
(Casino Locations)

Essential 52 Restaurants Index
(Non-Casino Locations by nearest major cross streets)

All Restaurants Index

All Restaurants Index

All Restaurants Index

All Restaurants Index

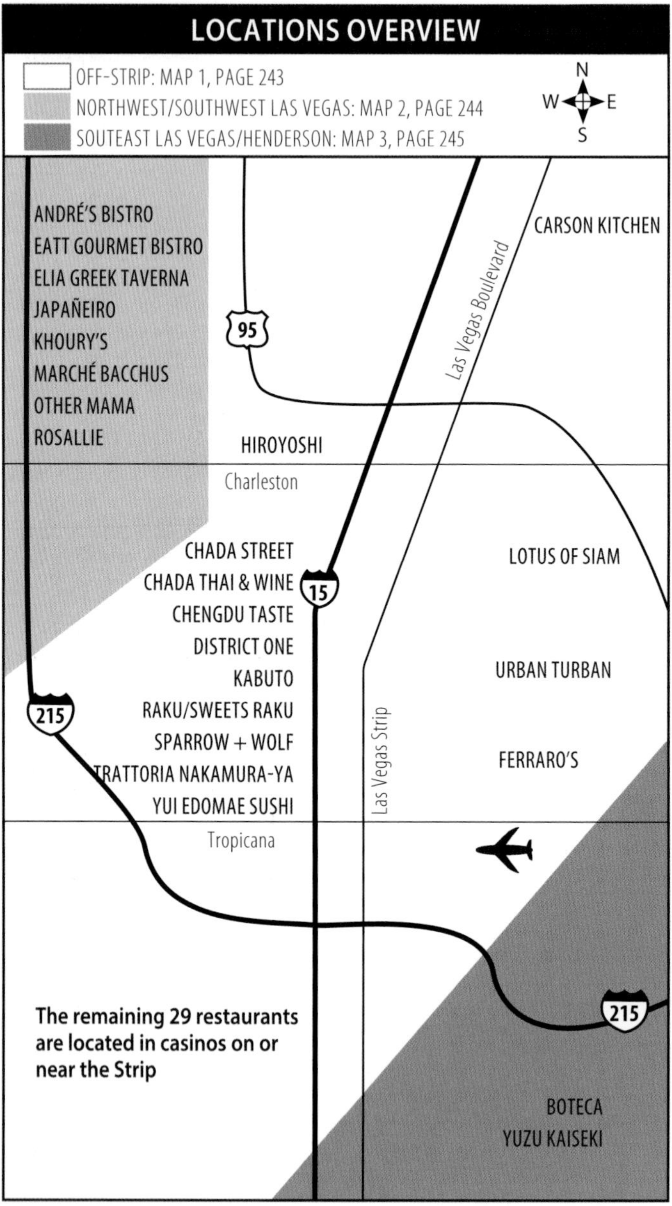

LOCATIONS OVERVIEW

OFF-STRIP: MAP 1, PAGE 243
NORTHWEST/SOUTHWEST LAS VEGAS: MAP 2, PAGE 244
SOUTEAST LAS VEGAS/HENDERSON: MAP 3, PAGE 245

N
W E
S

ANDRÉ'S BISTRO
EATT GOURMET BISTRO
ELIA GREEK TAVERNA
JAPAÑEIRO
KHOURY'S
MARCHÉ BACCHUS
OTHER MAMA
ROSALLIE

95

Las Vegas Boulevard

CARSON KITCHEN

HIROYOSHI

Charleston

CHADA STREET
CHADA THAI & WINE
CHENGDU TASTE
DISTRICT ONE
KABUTO
RAKU/SWEETS RAKU
SPARROW + WOLF
TRATTORIA NAKAMURA-YA
YUI EDOMAE SUSHI

15

215

Las Vegas Strip

LOTUS OF SIAM

URBAN TURBAN

FERRARO'S

Tropicana

215

The remaining 29 restaurants are located in casinos on or near the Strip

BOTECA
YUZU KAISEKI

OFF-STRIP, MAP 1

Fremont Street
Rainbow Boulevard
Jones
HIROYOSHI
Decatur
Valley View
15
Las Vegas Boulevard
CARSON KITCHEN
Charleston
Sahara
LOTUS OF SIAM
CHADA THAI & WINE
YUI EDOMAE SUSHI
Desert Inn
DISTRICT ONE
Paradise
SPARROW + WOLF
KABUTO
Spring Mtn.
CHADA STREET
RAKU
Sands Ave.
TRATTORIA NAKAMURA-YA
CHENGDU TASTE
URBAN TURBAN
Flamingo
FERRARO'S
Swenson
Tropicana
Las Vegas Strip
Paradise
Robindale

NORTHWEST/SOUTHWEST LAS VEGAS, MAP 2

NEARBY CASINOS: ❶ RED ROCK RESORT, ❷ RAMPART, ❸ SUNCOAST

SOUTHEAST LAS VEGAS/HENDERSON, MAP 3

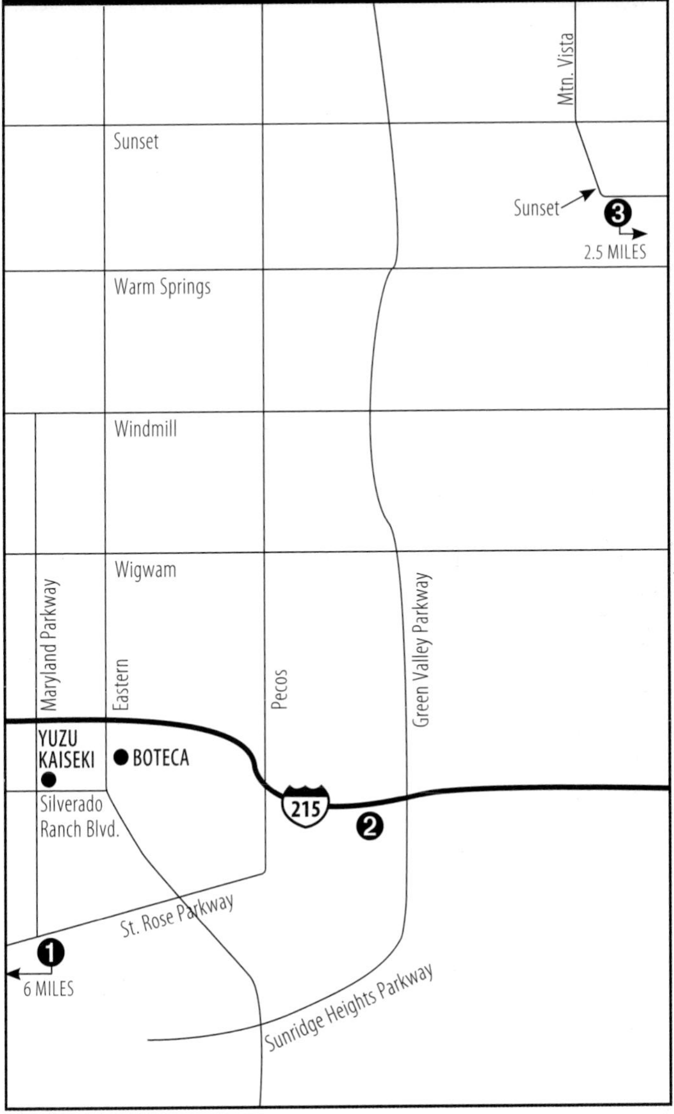

Mtn. Vista
Sunset
Sunset
2.5 MILES
Warm Springs
Windmill
Wigwam
Maryland Parkway
Eastern
Pecos
Green Valley Parkway
YUZU KAISEKI
BOTECA
215
Silverado Ranch Blvd.
St. Rose Parkway
6 MILES
Sunridge Heights Parkway

NEARBY CASINOS: ❶ M RESORT, ❷ GREEN VALLEY RANCH, ❸ SUNSET STATION

About the Author

JOHN CURTAS has been covering the Las Vegas food and restaurant scene since 1995. His "Food For Thought" commentaries ran for 15 years on KNPR Nevada Public Radio, and these days he can be seen every Friday as Las Vegas' "Favorite Foodie" on KSNV's (NBC) Channel 3's "Wake Up With the Wagners." He has written reviews for more magazines and guidebooks than he can count and has appeared multiple times as a judge on "Iron Chef America" and "Top Chef Masters." In addition, he also authors the Eating Las Vegas food blog (www.eatinglv.com). This sixth edition of this book, and the first with John as the sole author, reflects his 31 years of eating in more restaurants, more often, than anyone in the history of Las Vegas.

About Huntington Press

Huntington Press is a specialty publisher of Las Vegas- and gambling-related books and periodicals, including the award-winning consumer newsletter, *Anthony Curtis' Las Vegas Advisor.*

Huntington Press
3665 Procyon Street
Las Vegas, Nevada 89103
LasVegasAdvisor.com
books@huntingtonpress.com